LIES, LIAR
AND THE LIONESS

LIES, LIARS,
AND THE LIONESS

By Sandi King Kramer

ISBN: 978-1-59684-942-6

Printed by Derek Press
Cleveland, Tennessee
All Rights Reserved

Why I Wrote This Book

Sandi Kramer is a friend, mentor, leader, and a REAL woman who is not afraid to step out and share her life with others. I have had the privilege of knowing Sandi for the past 18 years. We attended church together, and from there, I began to see her life role. She truly has a heart for young teenage and college girls. Because of her journey in life and the many things that she has experienced, I believe it is her mission to share her life and to share the love of our heavenly Father with them. Her heart and passion is to see young girls become godly women who do not have to find their identity in the things of this world, but to find their true identity in Christ. For those that have already lost their identity, she is a true mentor who is not just there for the moment, but for the long haul. Several years back when my husband and I were youth pastors at Westmore Church of God, she held an all-day girls event for us. My daughter, who was only in the sixth grade at the time, received deep ministry. She was given a bottle of oil that day that represented the Holy Spirit. Now at 23 years old, she still has that bottle of oil. At the same event, my youngest daughter who was in elementary school also attended. She was given a little princess crown. She too still has that little crown tucked away as a memory to keep forever. To this day, both of my girls love and respect Sandi. My youngest, just the other day, told Sandi that she wants to be just like her.

Robert and I now work for Fellowship of Christian Athletes. One of the events that FCA sponsors is the P31 Girls Conference. The purpose and goal of P31 is to present to these girls the privilege and challenge of learning and living out biblical womanhood in all areas of their lives by teaching Proverbs 31. We want to address worldview issues with which women struggle today. Sandi does exactly that. Sandi Kramer possesses a deep level of spiritual and emotional maturity. She has always been the one we seek out when we are in need of someone to speak into the lives of young women. She gives wise counsel. She cares for others. Last year, she was our speaker for the P31 and again this year. Without any reservations, Sandi is and will always be a top candidate for being a lead speaker. I appreciate her being real with our girls, and I know that the young women feel the same. Young women today are looking for the real deal. They don't want fake, and Sandi does not do fake. She is an extraordinary woman who performs with excellence in every area of her life that I have witnessed. She has a joyful spirit, a passion to serve, a call to discipleship, and a heart to love any and every young woman that comes into her life, no matter what their story may be.

—Teresa Green
FCA Administrative Assistant, Ocoee Region

A few months ago, I realized a deep wound in me. I also realized that throughout my life I had been covering up this deep wound with different Band-Aids. When I came to the realization of the need to be healed from the wound, I sought out a life coach. I knew that I needed help to be able to begin my journey of healing.

I chose to receive coaching through Sandi Kramer. She has significantly helped me to be able to begin healing. The first thing Sandi helped me notice was my pattern of negative thinking. Naturally, I am a person who thinks a lot. As a result of my thinking, I tend to see the negative rather than the positive. Thinking a lot is not a bad thing; however, in my case, I was failing to see almost anything positive. Thus, I never was able to propel myself out of a negative situation. In other words, because I had a pattern of negative thinking, I could never take hold of a possible positive situational outcome.

Sandi has been an outlet for me to share my deepest, honest thoughts involving my hurts. She has positively listened and given me feedback on my thoughts, which I have appreciated. Unlike a family member or friend, I think Sandi provides an honest outlet of feedback. Along with giving me feedback, Sandi has also challenged me by giving me mini assignments and by calling out my negative thoughts. I have realized that by my thoughts being challenged, it has caused me to think about how a situation really stands. I feel that perhaps the most important challenge Sandi has offered is to spend time with Jesus. Honestly, I wasn't quite ready to spend time with Jesus when I first started receiving coaching from Sandi, but now I think getting back to Jesus is the most important thing.

—Nick Smith

Sandi Kramer is a wonderful human being. I first heard her testimony in a course I took a while back at Lee University. When I listened to her story, I realized the power that it held and how much I knew she could change the lives of women. I didn't know it at the time, but I thought the Lord was using her for my friend; instead the Lord was really preparing me for her guidance. She has been such a wonderful influence among the pain, emotions, heartache, despair, and restlessness. Sandi Kramer is a woman who fears the Lord, and she is going to radically change the world. I'm glad that she could radically change my world.

—Emily Gruner

Sandi Kramer came into my life at a time when I was broken beyond recognition. I didn't know the girl looking back at me in the mirror. I thought I was unlovable and had too much baggage following me around to ever be useful to anyone. We were introduced through Lena Barber, and I knew from the moment she came in the room that she was someone I could trust. She is shrouded in God's presence, and one can't help but be pulled into the light and peace she embodies. Through the years we've been meeting, Sandi has helped me work through my myriad of issues. She reminded me that I was worth the world to God by never giving up on me. Day or night, I could call and it never was a burden. She has helped me to become the woman I am today. I can confidently look back at the girl I was when we first met and compare her to who I am now, and say that without Sandi's guidance, I wouldn't be strong in my relationship with Father or believe that I am capable of the plan He has for me. She is the greatest blessing I've ever encountered and I will never come close to thanking her the way she deserves.

—Alexa Wallace

Sandi Kramer has been the greatest gift Father has ever blessed me with. Without her guidance, her influence, her unconditional love, prayer, and support, I can honestly say, I do not know where I would be today. Sandi is honest, raw, and real. She bares her heart and shares her life story with boldness, and that is what makes her the perfect mentor. I have found it easy to share the darkest details of my past with her, because she loves like Jesus and never casts an ounce of judgment. She is my accountability. She taught me that Father has feelings, and I would hate to ever do anything to hurt those feelings or to disappoint Him. In the same way, Sandi is so important to me, that I would hate to do anything to disappoint her as well.

Sandi taught me the difference between a saint and sinner—the saint always gets back up. Sandi helped me discover the good in myself, and because of that, I am a saint who gets back up! My failures don't define me, because failure is an event, not a person.

Sandi has taught me how to have a relationship with my Savior. She showed me the love my Father has for me and revealed the simple truth that all He wants from me is to love Him back. Because of the example she leads, I now know how to do that. I now know what a genuine woman of God looks like—it looks like Sandi Kramer.

The Lord speaks to me through Sandi. He has used her to remind me, on numerous occasions, that He is a God who sees me: That He is for me and that He just simply wants to be my best friend.

Sandi has walked alongside me on my life's journey for two years now and I thank my sweet Savior every day for entrusting me to her! Father speaks to her in such a beautiful way, and the relationship she has with Him is one I strive for. I have never seen someone with the level of respect or admiration for our Savior that Sandi possesses. Her heart has always been to walk through life alongside girls, teaching them how to love our Father back. Every conversation I have with Sandi teaches me something new. She is helping me grow into the person God created me to be. I love and admire her so much.

—Megan Wallace

I hope somehow this book inspires you to seek help if you don't know your personal truths.

—Sandi King Kramer

Gratitude

Thank you, Rick Kramer, for always believing in me and seeing the best in me. Thank you for allowing me to have vision; to inspire and write with my heart; and to encourage others to fulfill their dreams. You have my whole heart.

Thank you, Mom, for being such an inspiration to me, and for teaching me how to give, love, and try to be like Jesus. I am grateful you never gave up on me...
You make me brave.

Thank you, Gail, for putting up with me when I would annoyingly follow you around. I will always be your fan.

Thank you, God, my Father, for giving me, Ryan, Andrea, Lacey, Brandon, Reagan, King, Bri, and my grands. I am so grateful you picked me to be their momma and "grams, grami, and gramzie."

And to you, Lena Barber, thank you for allowing me the honor and privilege to speak into the lives of your students. I am so grateful for the memories we share forever.

Thank you, Roy Edwin King, my daddy. I get to see you soon. I know you will meet me at the gate.

Do I Like Peas?

There was a little girl, who had a disease to please,
She would even ask her sister, "Do I like peas?"

A chameleon she would be in the midst of the crowd,
Please, please can I just make somebody proud?

I just wanted to be accepted: "Do you really like me?"
I don't know who I am. Will you please tell me who I'll be?

In a still quiet voice, her heavenly Father would say,
"You're my sweet baby girl, please trust and obey.

"You are my modern day Esther, the one I love,
You are forever accepted from your King above.

"I've held you and nurtured you through your faceless years,
There's always been a place in my heart you have held so dear.

"I gave you my Son; my Spirit dwells within you,
You are my chosen vessel; I choose to work through."

My identity no longer is in the approval of man,
Jesus is my solid rock, with Him I can stand.

Nestled in the arms of my Father above,
I'm safe and secure, accepted by my Beloved.

—Sandi King Kramer

Table of Contents

14

Chapter 1

Liar

An adorable, cute, pig-tailed little girl came up to me crying while I was speaking at a youth service one night after I told my story. My heart broke with compassion as we began to talk. I asked her, "What's wrong? Why are you so sad and crying?"

With tears streaming down her beautiful, innocent face, and wiping them as quickly as they rolled down her cheeks, she said, "I'm so ugly."

Ugly was the furthest thought from my mind, so I asked her, "Who told you that?"

She responded, "My daddy."

I pulled her close to me and hugged her tightly as if she were my own, trying to console her shattered heart. I started crying with her, as I felt her heart beating out of her chest. My heart was broken for her. She was only 12 years old and dealing with such horrible rejection from the one with whom she was supposed to feel most secure. I can still see her precious face, and I pray for her as often as her name comes to mind during my time of prayer.

How can it be that, someone so full of hatred would speak such horrible, impressionable words to such a young, beautiful, and spirited child? I don't understand humanity. The words, the lies that were spoken over her—the Enemy of her soul will use them against her, rehearsing them in her mind as she matures into her adult life. If she doesn't have the tools to know how to cope with her private pain, she will believe the lies.

We believe lies that have been spoken over us every day, whether we like it or not. Until we take captive the thoughts that corrupt our minds with unworthiness, our self-image and self-esteem will act out the way we feel. Self-image is the way we see ourselves; self-esteem is the way we feel about ourselves. We then begin to act out what is dictated in our thoughts.

Image is not just a girl issue. Young guys, and men, battle the same challenges, perhaps just differently. Have you ever looked in the mirror and thought you looked good? Or maybe you woke up feeling ugly about your appearance; you even looked in the mirror with disgust and said: "I'm too fat or too skinny. My hips are big. My hair is too short and thinning. I wasn't raised in the perfect family. My daddy doesn't love me, why would anyone else? The man of my dreams walked out on me and left me for another man?" We all have our individual issues we deal with on a daily basis. In my early years of life, I didn't handle it as well as I do today. So be encouraged if you are in the struggle, there is hope and healing for you.

We compare ourselves with others constantly. If we allow them to, magazines will dictate to us the image we should portray. What we don't realize is the fact those pictures were probably altered to look amazing. All the while, we look at them thinking they are perfect, and we aren't. I know we shouldn't compare, and if you don't, great; but if you do, like me at times, don't feel abnormal. I am a "be real or no deal" kind of girl. Some things I say in this book you probably won't like, but at least I'm honest and will always speak the truth.

So here it goes . . . some truths. I am that wife who asks her husband to look at a woman's booty whether we are in the mall or on the beach. I will say, "Babe, does my butt look like hers? Be honest!"

And Rick's response is, "Is this a trick question?"

We all deal with a self-image issue in some way. For example, I don't see myself the way others see me. I overcome my insecurities by rehearsing the words my heavenly Father speaks over me daily. I do mean daily; sometimes hourly. I am His beloved, and He is mine. I know I am His blameless bride, but like I said earlier, it hasn't always been this way. I am still a work in progress. Philippians 1:6 says, "Being *confident* of this, that **he who began a good work** in you will carry it on to completion until the day of Christ Jesus" (NIV). I knew about Jesus and His love for me, but I didn't know how to live with Him. I pray that somehow through this book, you will begin to look deeper into the windows of your soul to see what truly is beyond the lies—a beautiful you.

I will tell you more about my family later in the book; however, my youngest son is named after my daddy, Roy Edwin King. Since King is my maiden name my husband felt it was appropriate to name him King. Name your child with destiny and purpose. If you don't know the meaning of your name, I encourage you to look it up. It's very interesting.

Back to King's name: he ruled our household in more ways than one. We hadn't planned to have children since we were a blended family and married later in life. However, God had a greater plan and knew we needed a baby King—our "surprise" child. I had planned to have a tubal ligation in June of 1992, but he was conceived in May. He is truly an amazing young man who not only loves Jesus with his whole heart, but lives Jesus out loud, too. He is a great son. Sometimes, I wonder how in the world he is mine. Trust me; I have the scar to prove it.

King was about six or seven when he invited a few of his friends over to spend the night. He was always a "homebody" kind of child. We were fine with that because his brother, Brandon, would call at 1:00 or 2:00 in the morning to pick him up if he were spending the night at his friend's house.

Our shower in that house was upstairs right beside King's bedroom. When I opened the door, I looked in his room and they were playing Xbox, laughing, and having a fun time, when I said, "Boys, do you know how great you are?"

King's immediate response was, "Mom, if you tell us one more time how great we are. . . ."

I thought . . . well, I guess he knows, since it's getting on his nerves.

Maybe you didn't have a parent, close relative, teacher or mentor to tell you that you are great. So, let me be the one to tell you. Greatness is within you. Stop right now believing the lies spoken over you. Don't allow one more minute to be robbed from you by believing the lies. If we are made in the image and likeness of our heavenly Father, and He is great, then greatness is within you, too. Every time you put yourself down, you are telling your Creator you aren't good enough. You are telling Him you don't think He did a very good job in creating you. Look around; see the beauty of His creation—the mountains, the hills, the beach, the sky, the stars, and all the many wonders of the world. Sometimes, life and all its "stuff" has a way of convincing us differently, covering up the beauty within.

Frequently, as a life coach, I am told: "I don't really know if God exists. And I'm just not sure what I believe." Well, let me ask you, "What have you created besides chaos?" Humanity creates the environment of rejection, insecurity, resentment, bitterness, and hate. God, the Creator of the universe, created you for the single purpose of love. It is humanity and our surroundings that sometimes speaks louder in our lives, rather than the still small voice that is saying, "Come, taste and see that I am good." Once you've tasted of His love, you will never be thirsty for what man can offer.

Since I am that "be real or no deal girl," I don't mind sharing with you my personal lies, because I now know my truths. One of the lies I believed for a very long time was that no one would ever love me.

Growing up, I didn't even know what the word dysfunctional meant. Through the years, what I have learned is that everybody has some kind of "funk" in their family. Dysfunctional families originated from the disobedience as described in Genesis in the Garden of Eden. Everyone played the blame game. Eve blamed her actions on the serpent; Adam blamed his actions on Eve. No one wants to take personal responsibility for their individual actions. Jealousies, murder, hatred, lies, were all lived out loud from that moment of deception.

I was raised where dreams come true. I lived in the world of, "Father Knows Best." That was a TV show much like, "Leave it to Beaver." I know what you are thinking—"old school." These were shows in the late 1960s and early '70s. If you have ever seen these shows it would depict my family. Mom would have dinner on the table at 5:00 p.m. when daddy came home from work. At least, the days he wasn't traveling and preaching. My older sister, Gail, and I had to do our homework after school, before we could turn on the television. I have great memories of my childhood and realize how blessed I was the older I get. However, I also realize other people weren't as fortunate as I was. My transition between the teenage years of 16 to 18 is when my troubles began. I soon realized everything people told me wasn't always the truth; some were absolute lies.

Liar

I remember coming home from high school one day, and I couldn't find my mom or dad anywhere. I looked all through the house. I went next door to the offices where my parents worked. I couldn't find anyone. I thought, *Oh no, Jesus has come and I'm left behind!* I was so afraid. Frantically, my mind began racing trying to think who I could call to see if they were still here. Suddenly, I thought, *Well, I know who I can call—I will call my pastor.* Then I thought, *Nope, can't call him; I think he is having an affair with someone in the church.* I know that sounds horrible . . . and it was. But, sadly, it was true. I was soon relieved when finally, my mom walked through the door. That is a horrible feeling to think you won't spend eternity with Jesus. Thank you, Jesus; I don't have to fear that anymore. I am saved by grace.

I am a PK—a preacher's kid. I was taught to live by rules that were seriously unrealistic for me. I am a free-spirited kind of girl. So, when I realized I couldn't live up to perfection, I gave in to my own selfish demise. Now, looking through the lens of a parent, I understand Ed and Sylvia were only doing their best, and they were amazing parents. People would criticize and judge us for our every move if it looked like sin to them. It was like living in a glass house where people would throw stones of judgment. I remember one incident; my sister was wearing a ring—a plain ring. And because it went against this person's belief system, or denomination, to wear rings other than a wedding band, my daddy was harshly scolded and instructed it wasn't holy. Daddy would always protect us from other people and their self-imposed convictions, but sometimes it was a bit much to grasp while watching the windows crack in the glass house, as church people threw stones. I am grateful to God those days of trying to please everybody are over; however, I do believe in pleasing my heavenly Father and doing what is right in his eyes. That is what truly matters—that is my truth.

God has been so merciful to me. Psalm 25:7 says, "Do not remember the sins of my youth and my rebellious ways; according to your love remember me, for you, Lord, are good" (NIV).

After my sister left for college, I was lost. If you have read my book, *Identity Theft: Who's Behind the Mask*, you have already read my story, but perhaps you haven't, so I must share with you, my stuff, my rebellious youth, and my lies.

I grew up quickly because my sister was four years older, and I wanted to do what she did. In fact, I was her shadow. I'm sure I got on her nerves, wanting to hang out with her and her friends all the time, but she was all I knew. I wasn't the little girl who played with dolls all the time; I followed my big sister, idolizing her every move. My first kiss from a boy was when I was 12 years old. We went on a double date with my sister and her boyfriend. I was way too young. I had on lip-gloss that tasted like soda—7Up to be precise. I wanted to make sure if he kissed me, my lips tasted sweet. It's funny the things you remember from your childhood.

My family would travel every two to four years, so once I would get the hang of making new friends, we would move to another city, state, or even country. My parents and sister were my friends. I have no regrets, because I am who I am today because of my experiences. I never meet a stranger. Everyone is my friend. Our family would travel on the weekends. Daddy would preach, his favorite girls would sing right before he spoke. So, you can mentally picture this family of mine. Mom would many times dress my sister and me alike. Since Daddy didn't have boys, Mom would sometimes make a matching tie for him so he wouldn't feel left out.

I love the fact that my family was very close. But, my world was rocked when my sister decided to move away for college; I was devastated. I didn't have a clue who I was, what I liked, what I didn't like or even if I liked something as ridiculous as peas. I will explain.

One summer we came home from living in Europe, so my sister could get her driver's license and to spend time with our grandparents. My sweet grandmother asked me if I liked peas. My honest response was, "Gail, do I like peas?" She said, "No, Sandi, you don't like peas!" I was 12 years old, naïve, ignorant, and unlearned in life; I was so sheltered I didn't even know if I liked peas!

Please, if this is you, discover yourself, your uniqueness, your individuality and allow your children to do the same—even if it means failure. You learn more about yourself through failure than success. I am proud to say, "I like sugar snap peas." I finally realized I have the freedom to make choices. Some of my choices, as you will read, weren't so good, and then again, some were absolutely fantastic.

When we moved from California to Tennessee after I graduated from high school, I was set to attend Lee College (now Lee University).

I had cheered all my middle school and high school years. My AYA cheerleading squad won all Europe in Spain. And I once cheered for the 49ers, because my high school squad placed third in the state of California. I thought I was big time then, so I thought I would give it a chance in college. At least, I could do something I knew I was good at in a "foreign land" called, the South; at least it seemed like that to me. Although I was born in South Carolina, we moved to California when I was just 3 years old. I had by now a West Coast mind-set.

Dad's position changed from overseer of California in our denomination to superintendent of Northern and Central Africa. Moving from the West to the Bible Belt South was a culture shock. I found out quickly, my clothes didn't fit this southern culture, and neither did my attitude. A guy I had been seeing since I was 13 years old, "my puppy love," moved from California to Cleveland to attend the same college. I thought fate was following me. We lived in Europe at the same time and moved to California at the same time too. I thought he must be my soulmate. My "puppy love" turned into my "first love."

I didn't struggle with drinking or drugs in high school; I struggled with me. I didn't know me; therefore, I fit into whatever mold or crowd that wanted me or I thought needed me. I just wanted to be accepted and loved from the world like my parents loved me. That's all I knew. However, I soon realized that was a fairytale. It wasn't long until I had developed a "disease to please." I was willing to please whoever and whatever to make them happy at my expense. It's crazy how we will endure our own private pain at the expense of offending someone else. Regardless of what hurt transpired to me, I wanted my first love to love me back. I wanted to take his breath away every time he saw me. I wanted him to want me, and no one else.

There is a reason to clarify our history in our relationship. We were very young, 13 and 15, and our families lived in Europe at the same time. At 16, we moved from Europe to California; so did his family. That is why I thought fate was following me. He began to seem interested in me in a more serious way. I was flattered. I was crushing, and I thought he was cute. He played basketball very well and there is something about an athlete that's hot. But I had to deal with my imperfections, including weight issues all my life, constantly feeling like I never measured up. He would come up on weekends to visit me, because he lived about three hours away.

I heard he was seeing someone else at the same time. Word travels fast in the church community. I thought he was supposed to be with just me. I learned quickly, that I didn't want to share him. She was beautiful and had the package. You know the combo—big breasts, booty, and long legs with no cellulite. Here I was, chubby and shorter. Jealousy got the best of me. When I found out he was interested in her and not flattered by me anymore, I decided to take matters into my own hands.

I manipulated him to come to my house for the weekend. It was a New Year's Eve. My bedroom was in an attic and had an entryway through the garage. He would stay up there, and I would stay downstairs. This particular weekend I had made plans for him. I thought if we would have sex that would seal our fate.

My plan was to set my alarm clock for 1:00 a.m., quietly pass my parents' bedroom, sneak upstairs to sleep with him until 5:00 a.m. the next morning. Then, quietly sneak back down the stairs, pass my parents' bedroom and go to sleep, acting like I was a sweet innocent little angel. The problem was I had to make it down before my mother would get up to pray at the crack of dawn. This night was different. I had decided I would convince him to do more than just sleep together. Since I heard he and this "girlfriend" were having sex, I thought I would convince him that I was better at sex than she was, and he would never want her again. He would be mine alone.

I remember him saying with conviction: "We shouldn't do this." Seductively convincing him otherwise, I said, "Oh yes, we should." I followed through with my sneaky, selfish plot to have sex with him. All I got in return was rejection and an eating disorder. I guess I wasn't that good.

When I realized, I wasn't good enough to keep him from wanting "her," I internalized my guilt and abused my body by taking up to 16 laxatives in one dose, many times. Throwing up to feel thinner, pulling my hair out in large handfuls, I thought if I could just be like "her," he would love me. It didn't matter how hard I tried, I couldn't measure up to her perfection. Comparing me to her was killing my mind, body, soul, and spirit. The voice of shame was screaming loudly in my ears.

My lie was, "you will never be good enough; no one will ever love you." My truth was Jesus loves me just like I am; I am worth dying for (John 3:16). Jesus died just for you, too.

Liar

Self-Awareness: The lies your Enemy has convinced you of become your personal truths. So, we must exchange those thoughts or lies with what God's Word says about you. For every lie, write out three truths the Word, the Bible, speaks over you.

For example: I didn't feel loved, and no one will ever love me back. That was my lie. Next, I researched three scriptures that speak the truth of how much God truly loves me.

Now, use the space below to write your lies and your personal truths.

Your Personal Lies:_____

_____
_____
_____
_____
_____
_____
_____

Your Personal Truths: _____

_____
_____
_____
_____
_____
_____
_____

Lies, Liar, and the Lioness

Chapter 2

A Sunday

The '80s were a struggle for me. Madonna came out with the song, "Like a Virgin," and I didn't fit into that mold either; another shame on me, I felt. When I graduated from high school, my life turned into the perfect storm; no, more like a tornado. When we moved to Tennessee and I didn't fit into this Southern society, I dropped out of college. (By the way, I had a paid scholarship; another shame on me.)

I never grew up saying or knowing what I wanted to do with my life. I never felt smart enough to be a doctor, lawyer, or politician; I just thought I would be a preacher's wife. My mom was a great preacher's wife. She loved my daddy. I knew I had a lot of love like she had, but I didn't know what to do with it. Obviously, I channeled it in the wrong direction—sex, which isn't true love at all.

I had been taught to manage money. I started working when I was 16. My first real job was working at Kentucky Fried Chicken. The first big no-no was when they gave me that red polyester uniform to wear every day. That didn't fit into my fashionable wardrobe. The second big no-no was when I pulled the biscuits out of the oven and I burned my upper arm. This job just wasn't for me. So after 12 long, laborious hours, I quit. I remember thinking about my image: *What if my cheerleader friends come in, where can I hide?*

Daddy was my money teacher. He taught me to budget my money by setting aside my weekly earnings. I would put paper clips around my dollars, so I wouldn't spend them and label them with a purpose. One label always had the word "tithe" on it. I was always taught it was better to give than receive; therefore, I wanted to make sure I was a giver. I guess I took that a bit too far when I gave my virginity away. I can laugh now, but it wasn't very funny back then. I'm sure Daddy didn't mean giving like that either. When I went to college, I always felt broke. I hated that feeling. The feelings of being out of control of what I wanted, but not having the money to buy it was horrible to me. I didn't have the smarts or the desire to work and go to college. I liked being independent. I wasn't in college for studying, but to socialize. And, that didn't get me good grades. If I could have received a grade for socialization, I'm positive I would have received an A+, even valedictorian of the class.

In the meantime, the guy I called my first love also left the same college, so I felt lost again. Most PKs from my denomination came to this college back in the day; it was like a huge youth camp . . . except it cost much, much more. My identity had transferred from my sister to him. What he said, I did. If he said smoke weed, I did. If he said snort this, I did that, too. If he said you're fat, I believed him. I began to believe the lies. The lies became my friend along with my best friend, ED—my eating disorder. I chose to make these decisions to gain his approval. He never forced me to do anything. I was always my own worst enemy.

In January 1982, I dropped out of college. A word to the ones who are in college now—don't quit. Keep focused and steady the course until you finish. But don't just go to waste money, either. Explore other options of what you like and don't like before you spend money you must pay back later, plus interest. Finding a vocation, a career path is okay, too. Just know what you love, and do it with purpose. If I lived with regret, it would have been to stay in college, earn my degree—a doctorate in psychology—then pursue a career in that field of helping people. Instead, God had another alternative plan for me in helping people, which I will share more about in later chapters.

In March of that same year, I received a phone call from my first love. My love for him had grown and developed from first love to true love, I thought. He had moved out of state, so when he called and asked if I would pick him up at the airport, the butterflies swirled. I was elated. I missed him. What we had was crazy love. We had been together for a long time, off and on, our families traveled the world. *Finally, he couldn't live without me,* I thought. I guess I was "that good." He's crawling back. I thought his call was my invitation back into his life, and I was in love with the idea of being in love. I just wanted to be loved, by someone besides my parents, and he was my familiar, first love.

My daddy and I were very close. I was my momma's girl until she didn't know how to handle me and my free-spirit attitude. I had a smart mouth and would try my mother's patience. I quickly became a daddy's girl. I looked up to him like he was my hero. At times, he would surprise me with paying off my bills; sometimes he would even break up with my boyfriends for me! I trusted him. I felt that if God ever needed to take a break, he could ask my daddy to sit on the throne and all would be right with the world. I needed him in my life. My daddy was "my everything"; he was my god. He was the only god I knew, and now my life was so messed up with my bad choices. I felt I had disappointed him so badly; I didn't know how to get back on track. I was in denial of what my personal truths were. I wasn't raised to be like this. This isn't the way my life was supposed to be. My life was spinning out of control. No vision, my destiny was completely on detour.

In chapter 1, I encouraged you to look up the meaning of your name for a purpose. When I discovered what Sandra meant; I was surprised but shouldn't have been. It means "helper of mankind." I wasn't fulfilling my name at all or, maybe I was, in a selfish, lustful kind of way. But I wasn't helping myself out of my own personal madness. In fact, I was perpetually falling into a pit, and I couldn't get out. I was dancing on the speakers of nightclubs to Donna Summer's "Hot Stuff" just to be noticed by someone. I loved to dance, but the church thought that was a sin; so, I shared my gift with the world that I thought would accept me.

This weekend was just another weekend where I would put the good girl mask on at home and leave it outside the door so I could pick it up when I got home. My mom said I acted like the devil with horns. As I stated earlier, we weren't very close during my rebellious years. Back then it wasn't funny at all. We laugh now because of our relationship—we are best friends. I can honestly tell her anything and she won't gasp.

I picked my first love up at the airport, checked into the closest roach motel, had sex all weekend, and anything else we could find called "fun" that was cheap. The three days went by quickly. I took him back to the airport, not knowing if I would ever see him again. My identity got on that plane, and I waved goodbye. My heart was sad, feeling empty and alone again.

My dad would travel months at a time to other countries. I thought I was hiding my world from him, but I guess my transparency got the best of me, or he had a direct line to God. What I know now was he did have a direct connection to God; he prayed and God listened. I received a letter from him from Africa prophetically instructing me I would be "with child," as daddy called it, if I didn't stop the lifestyle I was living. I still have that letter today locked away as a memoir and a miracle because of where God has brought me. I guess I wasn't hiding anything from my God. God told my daddy everything on me, to help save me. It was as if He knew me better than I knew myself. What a foolish thought. God created me, He knows me better than I know myself.

One morning I woke up feeling very sick and thought it was a kidney infection. When daddy would ask me if I was ok, I would say, "Sure daddy, everything is great, I'm fine." Actually, I was dying inside. I knew he could see it on my face, and my body was not healthy. My ED (eating disorder) had gotten the best of me, and my self-esteem and self-image were depleted. I was looking rough. I didn't care anymore about anything, or anyone. I was getting larger in size from the munchies after smoking weed and eating the whole bag of chips. My hair was falling out from ED, so I didn't have to pull it out anymore. I felt empty; I was a failure! So . . . I had chosen to be a failure at life, and that is all I could see. I was lost in more ways than one. Not only was my soul broken, but my spirit too. I had spent all my savings and now found myself broke and needing money. I decided to take a position at a local credit company. This one morning while at work, I felt extremely nauseated. I thought I had a virus. After a week of throwing up every morning, I decided I would take a pregnancy test. *Surely, there is no way*, I thought, *getting pregnant would never happen to me.* I was right. The test came back negative.

The sickness continued. After three weeks, I was getting concerned. I went to our local health department and took another pregnancy test, as they had suggested, but this one was a blood test. It came back positive. I was positively pregnant. I was shocked. Surely this can't be happening to me. I dodged this bullet once; I'm sure this test is wrong. I couldn't believe it. I began crying uncontrollably. I left the health department sobbing so badly I couldn't see the cars in front of me. My life was chaos, completely out of control. Thoughts were racing through my head about what I was going to do. I had disappointed my family so badly, now how could I face them? Oh, God, what now? I could run through red lights and pray someone hits me and I miscarry. Or, I could just run my car off a cliff and it would be an accident, then my family's name wouldn't be shamed.

I have an incredible heritage. My grandparents were the first missionaries to Cuba and India from our denomination. Recently, my mom returned to India to do mission work, flying into the city where she was born. It's crazy how life works in circles. It was a full circle for her.

Jokingly I say, I was living with the modern day biblical family. Father Abraham, Ed, was my dad; my mother was Sarah, and my sister, Gail, was Mother Teresa. I was the harlot of the family who couldn't keep her panties on—Rahab. So, what was I going to do now? The only thing I could do was take the matter into my own hands and abort this "thing" inside of me. There was no way I could attach feelings to this child because I was numb from the inside out. I didn't care what happened to me. I was a messed up little girl. I had to remove my sin from within me. That was my only thought, and I would never, ever tell a soul, especially my parents. This didn't match the mask I wore to them and their peers. My mask said I had it all together, according to their world . . . I thought. But I knew if I told the truth, disappointing my parents would be the worst of the worst. I felt I had disappointed them enough with not pursuing my schooling, no vision of the future. My sin was my secret. So, I called my close friend and asked her to help me find a place to abort my sin. She did. She scheduled the appointment on a Sunday. Really? A Sunday?

It was a normal Wednesday. That evening after work I came home to a surprise. As I mentioned to you earlier, our family was close. So close, that we would have family meetings. When I was younger our family meetings were called "King's Court." My daddy was always the judge, mom the prosecutor, my sister was usually, well let's just say, we would defend each other, depending on the circumstances. In this case, she was nowhere around, so I was on my own, I thought. I walked into the house only to find my dad had called one of his counselor friends to see if he could help get his baby girl back. I had changed so much; he didn't know how to get me back. This was his effort as my hero to try to rescue me. This King's Court family meeting changed me for the rest of my life.

My personal lies had gone too far for God's grace to reach me or save me from myself—or so I thought. What I know now is, His grace is sufficient for me daily, hourly, every second of the day. Grace gives us permission to call on Him whenever we need Him. My soul was screaming for help.

Self-Awareness: Take a few minutes and look inside the writings of the pages of your life and what do you read? What lie or lies has the Enemy of your soul told you and possibly convinced you so strongly they have become your personal truth(s)? Once you have recognized the lie, write out three truths the Word, the Bible, says about your lie.

Your Personal Lies:_____

_____

_____

_____

_____

_____

_____

Your Personal Truths: _____

_____

_____

_____

_____

_____

_____

Chapter 3

Guilty

The room felt cold. You could cut the tension with a knife. I am positive I brought the tension with me. I entered the living room, thinking, *I'm busted; I know it! God told him my secret, and now I have been found out.* Daddy asked me to take a seat. I felt like I was sitting in the electric chair about to die. I was to confess to my priest before my approaching slow death. I think that would have been easier than facing the truth. I was facing both men of God—double trouble for me—and Sylvia, my mom.

Just shoot me; a quick death would have been easier. I knew it was all over. This wasn't a normal King's Court. During all other family meetings, there were no visitors allowed. Daddy called this family intervention to order and explained to me why his counselor friend had taken a seat in this family courtroom. Daddy said, "I have asked my counselor friend to help this family, because all we want to do is get our baby girl back." I loved to hear my daddy call me his baby girl. My heart began to melt just from those words. I so desperately wanted to revert to my younger days when I was innocent. No guilty verdict ever entered a King's Court like the guilt I felt sitting in that chair.

As his lips were moving all I could think about was, when I was younger, how proud I was to be his daughter. It was like my childhood flashed before my eyes. When he would finish preaching, I would always go up to him after church, stand real close, put my arm through his arm proudly stating, "This is my daddy"; I belong to him. Now what I was about to tell him is going to break him. I wanted so desperately to lie. His expression of disgust toward me on his face was going to cause me to throw up. My proud declaration of being his daughter has now turned into a shameful disgrace.

As the family intervention continued, I began to realize my truths were going to kill him if I were to be honest. What nobody knew, in this room was, I had just come from the health department, hung the phone up from talking to my friend to schedule an abortion, only to be surprised by this intervention. God's timing was perfect. But at this moment, I didn't think so. My flesh wanted to run, but my spirit begged me to stay. I couldn't disrespect my daddy's wishes. It was confession time.

My mind began racing with excuses, searching for a way out of this confrontation. Confusion filled my thoughts, along with the chaos of how and what I was going to do. *Should I tell my truth? I can't, I thought, that will break their hearts too badly. What and who am I anyway? What have I become? I have become a harlot.* All I could hear were the screaming, accusing voices in my head saying, *"Sandi, yes, you are the harlot of this family. What a disgrace."* The voices kept getting louder. My heart felt like it was beating outside my chest. My mask was crumbling on my face. My mind would not shut up. The meeting continued.

Daddy was kind. His face showed concern and distress. The only thing I can remember was thinking: *How can I manipulate my way out of this one?* I wanted to escape, but I couldn't. I broke down and cried like a baby. Tears were streaming down my face. My life was a disaster—a train wreck headed for destruction.

In the past, my dad would always tell me, "Don't worry; everything is going to be all right." I was sure I wasn't going to hear those words this time. I had to be a big girl, pull my big-girl panties up for a change and figure this one out all by myself. The longer the meeting continued the fewer answers I had. My personal lies had caught up with me, and I was in the web. I was always taught confession was good for the soul, and my soul needed healing. So, I surrendered to do what was right. I confessed. Actually, it was more like purging. This time was a different kind of purging. I needed to get rid of and say all the stuff I had done over the past few years. As the words began to come out of my mouth, I couldn't believe I was "that girl." You know, the one you (we) made fun of in school—that girl who was looking for love in all the wrong places. She was the kind of girl you wanted to be with, but not take home to momma. Yeah, I had become "that girl."

Crying uncontrollably, I asked my daddy if I could sit on his lap, like old times when he'd hold me. Broken from my own self-inflected wounds, he opened his arms, pulled me close like his baby girl, and devastated, I crawled on his lap. I knew I had broken his heart with disappointment, but he kept his composure to try to not make me feel any worse than I already felt. That was just the way my daddy was to me. With my head nestled into his chest, I began to spill my truths. My life was a lie, and now I was a liar. I had to tell the truth. I must confess to them I had gone too far, and I didn't know how to get my life back. I didn't know who I was, much less, where my life was going—a straight path to hell. The pit was too deep, and I was buried in my very own coffin of sin. That's when I confessed to my parents. The counselor looked spellbound.

Daddy's prophetic letter had come to pass. With a trembling voice, tears of shame streaming from my eyes like a flood down my flushed cheeks, I said, out loud, "I am with child." I proceeded to tell my plan. "I have an appointment to abort this thing." There I said it. I couldn't believe the very words coming out of my own mouth. I continued to confess, my appointment for the abortion was this upcoming Sunday. The day I confessed was a Wednesday. He held me. He gently wiped the tears from my eyes. The room was quiet. It seemed like an eternity until someone would speak. The reality of my lifestyle was now his truth as his daughter.

I remember Dad sitting in the chair with me on his lap, the counselor sitting in the large chair, and my mom on the couch. Suddenly my daddy became "Jesus with skin on." In his comforting, sweet, tender, no judgmental voice, he said: "You aren't going alone; your mom and I are going with you." Even my mom was shocked. She was crying uncontrollably. He then made a statement that I get, now as a parent. You never want to see your child hurt with pain. He said, "Sandi, I wish you had never been born if you were going to go through so much hell. I so desperately want to take this from you. I would rather it be me hurting than you. I must have failed you."

Stunned from his response, I cried even harder. I thought to myself: "What? Father Abraham and Sarah are coming with me to abort their grandchild?" I was completely amazed, shocked, stunned, humbled,

35

surprised, and unworthy to say the least. All the adjectives could not even begin to describe what I was feeling inside. No way could I ever allow that to happen. All I could see was me at the abortion clinic, in a cold calloused clinical gown, with my legs in stirrups sprawled in the air, and my parents hearing their legacy, their grandbaby screaming as his body was being torn apart.

This was my lie, my sin. There was no way I was going to take them with me into the pit of hell. Yet, they were willing to go with me, so I wouldn't have to go alone. Sounds like my Jesus to me.

What father does that? It was then that I realized the love of my heavenly Father. Jesus became real to me. Jesus knew who I was and still loved me, even in my sin!

I knew God existed and Jesus was His Son; I just didn't know how to live with them and all my imperfections. The love my earthly parents showed me was unbelievable and unconditional. They didn't want me to suffer alone; neither did Jesus. When I think back to that day, I am still amazed at the love and mercy Jesus so graciously showed me through my loving parents.

On May 7, 1983, I married my first love. We moved away, and on December 14, 1983, delivered into my arms was a beautiful, healthy baby boy, 9 lbs. 10 oz. of love, my gift from above—Brandon Mychal Perritte. I knew when I looked into my baby boy's eyes, I was crazy about him. Life became new to me. I knew that I had to do whatever it would take to be a great mommy, like my parents were to me. How could I be so blessed to give birth to this beautiful gift God graced me with? He changed my world. I always tell him, I saved his life and he saved mine. This was the beginning of my great choices in life. My first great choice was accepting Jesus as my Lord and Savior. My second great choice was having Brandon. My third great choice is to come.

I believed lies, and now I had become a liar. Have you ever looked into the mirror and wondered," *Who in the hell are you?* I completely get you. I completely understand. That is why I have written this book. You no longer have to believe the lies and become a liar like me. There is hope for you. Your redeemer, Jesus, loves you more than you can even imagine, even in your shameful, sinful nature. Nothing takes Him by surprise. He knew you would reject Him, disobey Him, and betray Him, yet He loves you just like you are.

Guilty

Today is the day to declare, I will no longer believe the lies of man. No more will I be a liar. Today is your new mercy day. You must choose. No one can do it for you. Choose new life, not lies.

Self-Awareness: Take a minute and write out your lies. What lie have you believed for so long? Now write out your personal truths. Perhaps you too have dealt with rejection, an eating disorder, or maybe you have had an abortion, and you aren't sure where to go from here. Maybe you were manipulative and sneaky like I was, and you need to forgive yourself. Whatever it is, just be honest with yourself, this is your time to be real or no deal. Remember, for every lie, write out three truths the words of Jesus spoke about you.

Your Personal Lies: _____

_____

_____

_____

_____

_____

_____

_____

Your Personal Truths: _____

_____

_____

_____

_____

_____

_____

Chapter 4

Alone Again

Just because you're married doesn't mean you will never feel alone. You can feel alone in a room full of people. I was still learning about me, much less a new husband and a baby all at the same time. I was young when I got pregnant at 19 and married at the age of 20. I moved away from my parents and had to grow up very quickly. I didn't do such a good job. I made many mistakes in my marriage. I knew I loved my husband, but like my Savior, I didn't know how to live with him. I was still learning so much about life and all its "stuff." He was doing his best under the stress of life, and so was I. Our relationship was toxic. I brought out the worst in him, and he in me. So, after two and a half years, we decided it would be best to end the marriage. Too much life had happened, and we were going in different directions.

We were on and off for a long time, and now we had added a new dimension by having a child together. It was like we were all we knew, but yet we didn't know how to live with each other or without one another. So we decided to try it again after being divorced for nine months. In January 1987, we remarried. Unfortunately, we divorced again in August of the same year. It was finally over. I had lost my first love forever. Life got in the way of love.

I can remember asking my first love why he didn't love me, and he said he didn't know how. That's all I needed to know. I wish I had asked that question a long time ago, because I completely understood him now. I got it. He was raised differently from the way I was, yet we were both dealing with the same issues. It's called life and how to cope with our differences in a great big world. A child will never keep the marriage together. That is too much pressure placed on an innocent one who didn't decide to be here in the first place. It was a hard lesson to learn, but a valuable one.

That same pressure for a spouse to complete you is an unrealistic expectation as well. I hear that phrase and cringe. God is your Creator, and He is the one who has the power to complete you. If you are expecting that out of your spouse, you need to have a reality check. Man, is not your sufficiency; man, is fallible, but God is infallible.

As time passed, I was learning how to like myself, but I wasn't very successful at it. My focus was off me though for a change, which was good because it turned me toward being a great mommy; at least I was trying to be. What I know now is, if I don't invest in me, I won't be very good for anyone else. But in the meantime, I was still trying to find the real me; trying to break free from all the ideologies of what man says versus what I knew and had experienced about Jesus. I knew God loved me in all my mess, but I still had struggles. The great news is God loves me even in my struggles. My heart is eternally grateful.

After we divorced, I still struggled with sex. I didn't want the struggle, but the struggle wanted me. Sex was an approval for me, in a sick kind of way. Pleasing someone else, even momentarily, gave me value. I felt I had accomplished happiness, at least for one of us. I knew sex; I never knew intimacy.

I met a guy from college who was also a PK. He was dealing with a failed marriage, but showered love on Brandon and me. That was a big deal, because we weren't used to the attention, and he loved us both. We were a package deal. You couldn't love me without loving Brandon. He adored Brandon, and that was huge for me. We would visit him and he would leave me money on the counter to go spend on just us—a hundred dollars at a time. I was amazed; I thought that was the greatest thing. No one, except my daddy, had ever given me anything for just me, without wanting something in return. He affirmed me. I was beginning to believe his words, as he would tell me I was beautiful.

At times, I would catch him looking at me with a smile. I wasn't used to that, so I always wondered what he was wanting now. His love for me was genuine, and he began the process of putting my self- esteem and self-image back on the map. I was feeling really good about myself. My heart was being filled with happiness. I felt as if the pieces of my broken heart were slowly being put back together.

I remember sitting at the dinner table one day and laughing out loud. My dad's response was, "there's my baby girl again, she's laughing." I hadn't realized how long it had been. Sadness of life had consumed me, and I was trying to survive. Being a single parent, and the best one ever at that, was a full-time job for me. The struggle was real, but Brandon was my world. We were going to make it work, no matter what. My son wasn't going to suffer for my bad decisions. I was getting us on the right track when suddenly the rug was pulled out from under me . . . again.

This amazing guy who helped me so much wanted to introduce us to his parents because we were growing closer. We were talking of a future together—marriage. I was shocked by their Christian beliefs and actions. They said, "Absolutely not, she's just gone through a divorce and she has a child; leave her alone she is used goods." Rejected again.

Alone, just the two of us, my heart was broken, shattered to pieces. How could this be? They said they loved the same Jesus my parents showed me, but their actions didn't reflect the same way. Rejection tried to take root, but I fought it constantly, fighting the urge to embrace ED again. I missed this man tremendously, and so did Brandon. We had become close and were great friends, but we never saw each other again. I hope his parents are happy, because I am now. The journey continues.

As I mentioned earlier, sex was always my struggle. I may blow a few religious people's minds right now. I remember many nights after meeting another good ole boy on a blind date, and falling in love with him. We dated for two years. We had sex on Saturday night, and I cried out to God at church on Sunday morning to help me. I knew I didn't want to disappoint God again. But, I knew He completely loved me, even though He didn't approve of my behavior. He still loved me unconditionally.

I was learning about this word called *grace*. It was a new concept to me. I had a genuine heart after God. I repented from my bad decisions, but it was a daily struggle. Jesus loved me in my struggle, and I was trying to love myself. I will never be perfect. If I had to be perfect, then why did Jesus die on a rugged cross for me? That doesn't mean I don't try to please God. It's like this; when I hurt someone, and know that I have hurt him or her, I will immediately apologize to that person. That is the same in a relationship with Jesus Christ. When my actions disappoint Him, I apologize, and He accepts it with arms wide open, just like I do with my children. There isn't anything they could do to make me not love them or cause me to turn my back on them. I love them with unconditional love—the love my parents taught me—the love of Jesus. They were my example. But now the difference is that I have my own relationship with my Savior. He is mine, and I will try never to hurt Him intentionally. And if or when I do, and I'm sure I will, I will say, "I'm sorry." So, I am never alone anymore.

Do you feel alone? Have you experienced loneliness? Do you like yourself? Perhaps you feel abandoned, or suffer from separation anxiety. These are personal reflections that are beyond the lies that you've been told or have been spoken over you. Maybe your parents divorced, and you've watched them go through their personal torment. The Enemy of your soul wants you to feel alone and without hope. The word hope means "confident expectation." I wake up in the morning with hope. My confident expectation is in Jesus alone. I know He is with me and will never forsake me. I don't have to go through life alone anymore. And neither do you.

During the two years we dated, I learned much about myself. I learned what I wanted to become and what I needed to continually work on in my life and relationship with Jesus Christ. Some people come into your life for a season and for a reason. I knew my reason for this relationship—to find me.

Brandon and I had moved back into my parents' house after my second divorce to get back on our feet. One night coming home from being at this guy's house, I remember crying out to God, again. I came into my parents' house and built an altar. I remember reading about it in the Old Testament, and I thought if it worked for them, surely it would work for me. So, I was the sacrificial offering. I needed to change; I needed to be more like Christ. I was sick and tired of the fight within me. I visually recall a huge altar. I climbed up on that altar lying down on top of it determined to not get off until I was changed. I cried out, "God change me! Burn out of me everything that doesn't look like you." I can't recall how long that night was; but what I do remember is the fact that I was changed. My desires changed. My mindset changed. I decided that it was more important for me to please my Savior than my humanity.

What are you struggling with? God loves you in your struggle, but He loves you too much for you to remain the same way. Change takes discipline. I lacked self-control. You must learn how to discipline yourself in gaining self-control. You must want to change before change will come. You must be sick and tired of being where you are. You must want to move in the direction toward where God wants you to be— complete in Him.

What do you want God to change in you? Sacrifice your selfishness, your sinful nature, and allow him to burn away your humanity. He will exchange beauty for your ashes. Isaiah 61:3 says:

> . . . and provide for those who grieve in Zion—to bestow on them a crown of beauty instead of ashes, the oil of joy instead of mourning, and a garment of praise instead of a spirit of despair. They will be called oaks of righteousness, a planting of the Lord for the display of his splendor (NIV).

God delights in you. When I think about how much He really loves me, my mind can't comprehend it. To think the God of the universe chose to leave His heavenly home to take on the form of humanity, to feel hurt, pain, and despair, so He could relate to my hurt, pain, and desperation—I truly can't comprehend His love. But what I do know is that I will love Him back with all my heart, mind, soul, and strength.

Self-Awareness: What is it that you want to change about yourself? Perhaps you have a personal struggle; God knows and loves you anyway. Lay it on the altar. Let your selfishness and your human nature die, and allow God to live in you and through you. Perhaps you're fighting loneliness, or maybe you've listened to the lies for so long you can't see beyond the lies. Look deeper inside you. Write out how you feel and what your struggles are. Now, lay it down; take your grip off what seems familiar, and let go and let God take control. Miracles are instantaneous, while healing is a process. I have seen more healings than miracles. What I know is nothing is too hard for God. He can heal your brokenness. What brings you to your knees? What makes you cry from within from past lies? Write them out and replace the lies with what God says about you. He's crazy about you.

Your Personal Lies:_____

_____

_____

_____

_____

_____

_____

Your Personal Truths: _____

_____

_____

_____

_____

Chapter 5

"Please God, Don't Let Him Die"

The year was 1988. Brandon and I were still living in my parents' house. Dad was still traveling to Africa; Mom had now graduated from Lee College (now Lee University). She received her teaching degree, and I was trying to make something of myself, working at a travel agency. I loved to travel, but no way was I going to leave my baby boy for a career. We would face whatever life brought us, together. Brandon was going to start kindergarten in the fall, and I couldn't believe he was growing up so quickly right before my eyes. We were so close. You didn't see one without the other. He was my world, my focus.

I was 25 years old, discovering I needed God daily in every aspect of my life. Some days I felt successful in my relationship with God, other days, not so much. The word mercy is used in the King James Version 10,420 times and is the seventh most frequently used word in the Bible. *Mercy* means "compassion and forgiveness." When I read the Psalms, I completely understand David crying out to the God of the universe for mercy. The Bible says that His mercies are fresh and new every morning. I believe that scripture was written just for me. He knew I needed his mercy daily, sometimes every second of the day.

My daddy was still my god, but I was learning slowly how to live with my Jesus. My daddy was tangible. I could just wrap my arms around him, sit on his lap, and all was right with the world. I didn't quite understand at the time that I could do that with my heavenly Father as well. I would feel God in the form of conviction when I knew I hurt Him, but I knew I needed to know Him more. My heart was pure, but I was still trying to wrap my head around how that all worked. I was doing my best.

In February of 1988, Dad and Mom came home for Christmas from spending time in Europe. It was my first Christmas alone and probably one of the saddest of my life. Brandon spent Christmas Day with his dad who lived out of town. My heart was broken without him. However, I was grateful to have a friend, Darla Ledford Prater, at least to have a Christmas dinner with. Needless to say, neither of us were cooks. She is a great cook now, but back then, we were struggling. The chicken didn't cook long enough so we ate veggies, afraid we would get sick from eating raw chicken. But we had fun together, and that's all that mattered.

When my parents arrived home, I knew something wasn't right. Daddy didn't look right. His eyes were like sunflowers, or buttercups. So, he went to the doctor. Immediately, he was scheduled for routine gallbladder surgery.

Dad was a survivor. His childhood and family growing up wasn't always the greatest. He was trying so hard to not make the same mistakes like his parents. He tried very hard to balance his love for missions, people, and his family the best he could.

He was never sick. I can't recall him ever complaining of even something as small as a headache until he turned 50. He had a heart attack, and I always thought I was the reason because I had put so much pressure on him with my bad decisions and my choices in life.

I remember vividly, this one time when he went with me to the attorney's office for the first divorce. We sat patiently waiting for the divorce attorney to enter his office. The attorney started the conversation with, "Why do you want a divorce?" My dad spoke up and said, "I am so tired of my daughter being abused." Abuse comes in many forms, not just hitting. I take full responsibility in saying, I wasn't always right either. I am positive I provoked the abuse. I had a mouth on me; sometimes I still do. I know the words I spoke to him were just as mentally abusive. Brandon's dad was a good man. I could see what he could become, but I didn't think he could; and that made me angry. I wish I could have taken back all the grief that I caused my dad. My goal was to prove to him with my actions that I was going to make better decisions and not cause him any more pain. Oh, how I prayed I wouldn't.

During the divorce proceedings in the courtroom, I would discretely watch my daddy check his pulse. When they called my name, and as I approached the judge, I could sense his nervousness, mine too. There were a few times I honestly should have been in jail. I wasn't very comfortable standing before any judge, guilty or innocent. Dad never wanted me to hurt alone. He never, ever blamed me; I did that all by myself. Shame.

The day arrived for his gallbladder surgery, and the room was filled with people who dearly loved my family, waiting to hear what the doctor said. I will never forget that day. It is as fresh today as if it was yesterday.

The doctor entered the room. The door shut behind him. Unexpectedly, he looked at my mom and said, "Sylvia, Ed has pancreatic cancer." The room got quiet from shock. My mom fell to the floor crying out to God, "No, God, no!" She was sobbing uncontrollably. After some time passed, gathering her composure, the doctor proceeded to explain what happened during what he thought was a routine surgery. As they opened daddy up, they saw the cancer. The doctor, who was Daddy's friend, assured Mom with confidence they had removed it all.

After a while in the hospital, they sent him home to heal. Daddy was recovering slowly, but with his mission mindset, he was determined he would visit Africa again. By this time, he had lost a lot of weight. His faith could not be shaken as he continued to pray and believe he was going to be healed completely and return to his love—the mission field.

In June of that year, he returned to Africa. Mom was a schoolteacher, but she was out of school; so she would travel with him, not wanting him to be alone. She loved to be with him, but she also knew God had given her, her own mission field—teaching fifth grade in a local public school in our city. It was her passion and purpose. The school was in a lower economic community. She would not only teach the children, but she would also love on them.

When they arrived home, Dad just wasn't right . . . again. He ran a fever on the airplane and was sick to his stomach. Mom was preparing herself; she knew in her spirit something was wrong. She took him back to the doctor, but Mom and Dad kept fighting and battling in prayer for his health.

Dad loved to preach. It was his passion. His mission in life was to tell as many people about Jesus as he could, so they could make heaven their eternal home. In our denomination, they have what is called a General Assembly. Every two years, the people gather together, and make changes in church legislation, make assignments, etc. This was Assembly year. To preach at a General Assembly was an incredible honor. When they asked Daddy to preach, he was honored; he was beyond excited, he was elated. His purpose was in motion. To know his background would even magnify this honor even more. An Anderson, South Carolina, painter's son is now preaching at one of the church's largest gatherings—quite the accomplishment.

Daddy's health was quickly failing him. In and out of the hospital all summer long, months at a time. His body endured so much pain, and he was getting frail. Things weren't looking very good right now, but he insisted on traveling to Dallas to preach. Whenever Dad set his mind to something, it was hard to convince him differently. (I'm sure my hardheadedness came from his side of the family.) We knew only God could change the course of his decision, so we supported his dream. His mission was to deliver the word Jesus had given him to his fellow brothers and sisters in Christ. Who could argue with that?

When Dad was well physically, he was 160–165 lbs. 5 feet and 11 inches tall, and so handsome. But the sickness took a toll on his body, and his health was depleting, quickly. His face was drawn from losing so much weight. He was about 110 lbs. now. He wasn't looking healthy at all. Professing his faith, he was a fighter, a survivor. My heart was hurting for him. I held back the tears in front of him.

It was the Friday before he was scheduled to preach on Saturday night. Mom called the family and me into their room. Dad looked so bad, but I couldn't say a word to discourage his faith or crush his spirit. All I knew I could do was to believe with them that Dad would live and not die. My thoughts were screaming . . . *there is no way Dad is going to die, no way.* He is way too good and loves so many people. Dad would give the clothes off his back to anyone in need. In fact, a pastor in Africa needed a suit, so what did Daddy do? He gave him his suit before he left the country. Thoughts were racing through my mind, *Please, God, take me, not my daddy.* I'm the one who deserves to die. He is too good to die.

"Please, God, Don't Let Him Die"

Mom said when he would try to eat he didn't have any strength and couldn't keep anything down. His health and his ability to preach looked very grim. Unless we got a miracle, he didn't have the strength to preach, much less get out of bed. Immediately, we began to petition God: "God, you got this, right? Nothing is too hard for you. Just do it, God, heal him, please. Is this really too much to ask?" My thoughts were frantic with fear trying to comprehend this madness before me. *Remember all the good your servant has done? All he has sacrificed for the sake of the call?*

Saturday morning came; Dad had to be medevac'd back to Cleveland, Tennessee. This was the beginning of the end.

He was rushed into emergency surgery when he got back home. The family was anxiously waiting for the doctor to give the report from surgery. Who knew five words from the doctor would change our lives so drastically, forever: ***"Sylvia, the cancer has returned.*** It has consumed his body, and it doesn't look good. We're giving him six months to live." I was stunned, shocked, perplexed, broken, shattered, defeated—my mind reeled: *This couldn't be true; surely the doctor was mistaken.* This is a nightmare! Please, someone, wake me up.

Daddy was such a family man. All he asked was for his three favorite girls to come see him in the recovery room. The doctor had just told him the results from the surgery. We surrounded his bed. He was hooked up to all kinds of machines. Extremely weak from the trauma to his fragile, mortal body, Daddy addressed my sister at the foot of his bed. They had their moment of time. Mom, of course, would have lots of time in the next few months to embrace this journey of uncertainty. He looked straight at me, his baby girl. I leaned over to hug him. I will never forget the words he spoke to me.

With his breath failing him, softly he said, "Baby girl, this time Daddy can't tell you everything is going to be all right. Daddy is dying." It was a sad day for me, but glorious for my dad. On December 19, 1988, my daddy, my god, died. I just wonder what saint met him at the gate.

Self-Awareness: What are you struggling with? Perhaps you've experienced death, disappointment and despair, and you can't seem to get over your grief. Or maybe you're experiencing grief from a dying relationship. You knew you had heard from God that you were to marry or be with this person, and now this individual is no longer in your family portrait. My lie was that my daddy, my god, had died. I had to deal with disappointment, because I knew that God could have changed the outcome, yet he chose to let my daddy die. Jesus wants to speak life into your situation even when you don't understand His ways. It might be a business God is trying to birth within you for years; yet, you have suppressed it because of your previous failures. Whatever "it" is, write out the lies that you feel are dead within you. Get real with God, and God will become real to you.

Your Personal Lies: _____

_____

_____

_____

_____

_____

_____

Your Personal Truths: _____

_____

_____

_____

_____

_____

Chapter 6

But God, What About Me?

The funeral home where my daddy, my god, was lying in tranquility didn't seem real to me. I wanted to crawl into the casket with him. It is so hard for me to begin to describe what I felt that day. People were gathering around to support the family. In the distance, I could hear light-hearted laughter as if this were a joke or something. Parents allowing their children to run in such a somber, depressing place was unreal to me. I wanted to scream, "Stop it!" I thought, *surely I'm going to wake up from this horrible, despicable, haunting nightmare. How could everyone be carrying on, when my world was dead? My daddy was dead.* I knew I couldn't die, too; I had Brandon. I was reminded of what I have always told him, "I saved your life, and you saved mine." I couldn't begin to understand, nor comprehend, life without my daddy. I admonished myself: *Come on Sandi, get it together; life must go on.*

On the day of his funeral, when I glanced around the church for a fleeting second, people were packed in like sardines. I had never seen anything like it. It was standing room only. Saints from all around the world were there to honor Roy Edwin King. That little Anderson, South Carolina, boy was now standing, perhaps kneeling, before the throne of his Maker—the one he told strangers about all around this world for so many years. Ed King was now in His presence, whole, healed, delivered, and pain free. "But, God," I cried out, "what about me?"

When the funeral director closed the casket, the pain of not having my daddy with us anymore was worse than any mental or physical abuse, bruises, and heartache of both divorces. None could compare. All I could think about was how we, Mom included, were going to survive. Mom almost passed out from her grief-stricken, shattered heart. I had never, ever seen her like that. She was always so strong, but always supporting Daddy. A friend of the family stayed beside Mom and held her up from fainting as we mourned and followed the casket out of the church. I will never forget, in the middle of the funeral, she cried out sobbing uncontrollably, "No, God, no." I felt helpless. I couldn't change things, and honestly, the feeling of hopelessness was overwhelming to me as well.

My mom's identity was all wrapped up in Dad, his work, and his ministry. She felt alone. I knew the feeling of loneliness, but not to this extent. They had been married for 30 years. I never knew love like that. He was so young, only 53 years old. I have always heard that if you bury someone on a rainy day, it was God crying with you. It poured that day at the gravesite.

Daddy had bought a nice townhouse for Brandon and me to live in. We lived on our own now, but since Mom was living alone a few blocks away, in a big house, it was only natural for us to move back in with her. It was our way of trying to bring normalcy during her despair. I hated her new normal way of life. My heart was shattered into pieces watching her grieve the death of the love of her life.

I remember her first Valentine's Day without him. I couldn't celebrate love that day, because I was so concerned for her wellbeing. How could I be happy when my mom was so devastated?

Despair doesn't even begin to describe what happened the next five years. I asked Mom to write in her own words the story of her life during this time. Some of her story may sound a bit repetitive with mine because she explains from beginning to end her experiences from her perspective with Dad. Mom's story is called "Cinderella."

"Cinderella"

Cinderella has always been my very, very favorite fairytale. I can watch the different movie versions over and over. Every little girl wants to marry and have a "happily ever after life." She wants her "knight-king" in shining armor to pick her up, swing her around, and take her away to never-ending happy land!! Well, that took time in my case. Ed and I met at Lee College (now Lee University), and in a few months, we were married.

I came from a missionary's family, which now lived in Cuba. Ed came from what was considered a well-to-do family, though they would be considered dysfunctional in today's culture. Nevertheless, after many hard first few years of marriage, we learned to be friends with a wonderful relationship. Ed held many different positions in our church denomination that took us across the nation, as well as overseas. The last assignment was superintendent of Africa, which covered 32 countries. He would be gone for several weeks at a time, but usually with other ministers. He had a passion for his work; in fact, he cried many times when telling his experiences.

On one trip, friends of ours and I met him in Germany. When we met him at the Frankfurt Airport, I mentioned to one of my friends, Ed doesn't look very well. Ed rarely complained, but I noticed he ate very little and visited the restroom a lot, along with many sleepless nights. When we arrived in Cleveland, he visited the doctor for a checkup. The doctor scheduled him for gallbladder surgery. After more than seven hours, we were still in his hospital room filled with family and friends. The doctor finally came and announced to us that Ed had pancreatic cancer and only a short time to live. I fell on my knees crying and screaming, "Not Ed!" This was February 1988. Ed died at the young age of 53, on December 19, 1988.

My "knight-king" in shining armor that I lived with for 30 years who took me all over the world and treated me like a princess was gone forever!! I fell apart. I felt rejected, forsaken, confused, and I went into severe depression! Why God? I would walk sometimes for 6-9 miles a day on one of our main streets in Cleveland, screaming, "I hate you God," yet I could hear Him say, "but I still love you."

Through the years because of severe depression and deep grief, I became suicidal and tried to take my life several times over a period of 5–6 years. But, God still had a plan for my life. One day as I was walking, I asked God, "Why didn't you take me when I had an anaphylactic reaction to a bee sting and medication?" The doctors told Ed they had done all they could do for me, six months after I had Sandi, and it would take a miracle for me to survive. As you now know, I did and had a wonderful life until Ed died.

But again, sweet Holy Spirit whispered in my spirit, because I know his voice: "For I know the plans I have for you declares the Lord, plans to prosper you and not to harm you, plans to give you hope and a future" (Jeremiah 29:11 NIV). This verse from the Bible became my salvation for survival! He reminded me that He is a personal God. He needed to take care of Ed, but he hadn't forgotten me. He also reminded me when we were married He oversaw both of us as a couple! He had our best interest in mind always, even when I didn't understand His ways. However, I was still fighting depression daily, until one night about 10 p.m. Sandi came to my house. All I can remember was Sandi saying, "Mom, I'm tired of Satan robbing you of your joy and will to live." We both knelt on our knees in desperation, crying profusely and praying. I don't remember specifically what she prayed, but we both arose and she soon left.

Every morning before I would leave for school, when Ed was home, he would complement me and tell how much he loved me. Now that he was gone I would change outfits as many as six times before I left home. I hated life without Ed. I was frustrated, angry, and bewildered. It didn't matter what I did, I felt ugly inside and out. Also, every morning when I woke up after three to four hours of sleep, I would think of ways how I could end my own life. Yes, I wanted to die. Ed was given large doses of morphine to ease his pain, and it was still at my house. I battled just taking it and letting go of my pain of loneliness. I wanted to get rid of me. I didn't like Sylvia, and I didn't want to live with her.

On one morning, I was at school teaching math when suddenly I gasped loudly because I realized I hadn't thought about suicide before my feet hit the floor. The breath of God must have breathed on me in the midnight hour, because I had a newfound hope to keep persevering and run this race called life. I immediately left the room full of fifth graders and went to the teachers' lounge. I cried so hard my heart hurt, while another teacher covered my class until I regained my composure. What a miracle! From that time until now, I have not tried to take my own life. I would be lying to you to tell you that I never felt lonely, or depressed again, but it wasn't to the extent of not wanting to live. Firsts are always the hardest—first birthday, Father's Day, anniversary —and until this day, they are still hard. I remember how precious he was to me and how much he taught me about life. We grew up together; Ed was all I knew.

"But God, What About Me?"

Remember the Cinderella story? Knight in shining armor, sweep me off my feet, and live happily ever after? Well, it didn't end like that for me, the way I thought it would. Due to all the stress, internal grief, hate, anger, bitterness, inward strife, and unforgiveness I had stored up and kept in for so many years, I had a slight stroke that affected the right side of my body. I realized then I had to release those whom I needed to forgive, and let go of the bondage that was taking my life into captivity due to my feelings of rejection and self-hatred. I began walking through the grief process, accepting the challenge to live and not die and walk personally with my prince from Galilee named Jesus. He has so graciously given me a fulfillment of teaching school, and I can retire from devoting my life to students for 28 years. Now, I can walk others through their individual grief and loss of losing their identity, husband, and best friend. There is life after death. I am a living testimony of God's amazing grace and eternal mercy.

Yes, I still think of the love of my life, Ed King. Yes, at times it is extremely hard, but what I know is that I will one day get to see him again and live together for eternity. Until then, I have a great support system with new friends and a great family who loved me through my days of depression. God had to take me to the bedrock of my soul to help clean out the toxic things in my life I had accumulated through the years. Then, He started filling my life with Himself. He could handle my anger and hate toward Him. He understood my pain. Jesus has taught me through His Word what life is all about. It's about being so dependent upon Him that nothing else matters.

In the past, I was dependent upon Ed for my earthly needs, for which I didn't even have to ask my heavenly Father. Now, I am completely dependent upon Jesus to supply all my needs according to His riches in Christ Jesus. He lacks nothing. Daily, I ask for wisdom and direction where, in the past, I would seek Ed. All along, Jesus was asking me for a relationship to draw intimate with Him. Today, we have a relationship I never dreamed possible. My girls often remind me I am not the mother they were raised with. Even though I had to endure a horrific spiritual cleansing and the tragic loss of a great companion, God replaced the ugliness with good things in life, and I love myself and love living. I am His Cinderella!

My mother's courage and life is an amazing inspiration to me. I watched her go through her own personal tragedy and back. She survived. Depression didn't defeat her. I watched her nurture my dad through cancer that ate through the skin on his stomach that made sores. She would change the dressing on his wounds. She loved endlessly, and unconditionally. Many nights at the hospital she would never sleep, making sure his needs were taken care of before hers. She was devoted, for richer or poorer, in sickness and in health, and until death did they part. Eternally, they will live forever. A covenant is a promise, and she always taught me to never make a promise I was not able to keep.

My mother and I were close until my rebellious teenage years. I know now it was all me because of my attitude and stubbornness, but she prayed for me and never gave up on me, even when I had given up on myself. She helped mold me. Growing up, my mother would make breakfast for us, usually sausage and eggs, with grits. If you're not from the South, you just may have to try them for yourself. Add a bit of butter; that makes them better. She would prepare breakfast while we were getting ready for school. What I remember about those wonderful mornings was, she had a very small "daily bread" devotional loaf. In it were scripture verses. Our responsibility was to learn one each week. If we mastered it before week's end, she would give us another one. I always looked for the shortest verse. I wasn't sure if I could remember the long ones.

The nights I would dance on the speakers to Donna Summer's, "Hot Stuff," or Michael Jackson's "Thriller," I would hear those scriptures pounding in my head, as I would go to sleep. I knew my destiny was bigger than the speaker I was dancing on. I had a praying Mom and Dad who prayed me right out of hell! I'm so grateful!

Growing up, I never dreamed I would experience the death of a parent at my young age of 25. My daddy isn't here today to get to see me live my life complete with Jesus. Silly as it may seem, I hope Jesus lets him get a glimpse occasionally, peeking through the clouds of heaven just to see what an impact he made in my life. There isn't a day that goes by I don't miss him. But I know I will get to see him again soon! I'm sure he will greet me at the gate; this time with a friend. It will probably be father Abraham, since I always thought they were alike. Abraham was a father of many nations; so was my daddy.

Self-Awareness: Perhaps you can relate somewhere in this story. Perhaps you know what it is like to experience the death of a close friend or loved one. Maybe you don't have a good relationship with your mom or dad. What are some of the lies the Enemy of your soul has told you? Write out your personal lie, but don't leave yourself there. Take a few minutes and find the three truths from the words of our heavenly Father. Read Jeremiah 29:11; memorize it; rehearse it out loud; and realize God is not finished with you yet. He has a plan and a purpose for you to fulfill. It is time to walk into your destiny. People need for you to survive—their life may depend upon it. My prayer for you is to find your wholeness in Jesus Christ.

Your Personal Lies: _____

_____

_____

_____

_____

_____

_____

_____

Your Personal Truths: _____

_____

_____

_____

_____

_____

_____

Lies, Liar, and the Lioness

Chapter 7

Used Goods

Hardheaded, stubborn, determined, and having pure bulldog tenacity is what kept me alive, along with Brandon. If I were going down, it would be with a fight! I didn't grow up being an independent little girl in relationships. I was extremely dependent, but I had to learn independence after my sister left home and again after having Brandon. It was time for me to grow up if I were going to make something out of us. I knew if I would try to do what was right, God would honor this family even without a father figure. Daddy always called Brandon his champ. I sure wasn't going to let "the champ" be disappointed in his momma. We were a team.

After my second divorce from the same man, I realized I didn't make good decisions. Before my daddy died, I would incorporate his help. I remember vividly bringing guys over to the house to meet daddy. We would have dinner together. Daddy always sat at the end of the table. The plan was, if he approved, I would look at the end of the table and he would shake his head yes or no. I got more noes than yeses! Now that daddy was gone, it was time I learned how to make decisions on my own. I dated, but no one swept me off my feet like my mom's Cinderella fairytale. The one guy I thought was my fairytale husband, his family said I was "used goods." Well, that didn't work. Another guy I dated told me I wasn't "playboy material." So, he dumped me, too.

I didn't want to live life alone. In fact, I hated being alone. I battled my personal lies—"No one will ever really love you, now that you have a child and you aren't playboy material." I rebuked the lie, and trusted that God had a plan for me. I'm still not playboy material, and I am perfectly fine with that.

Although my decisions often took me by surprise, my decisions never took God by surprise. I never dreamed my life would look like this—twice divorced, single, and a child before marriage. However, God knew I needed my Brandon as much as he needed me to be his mom. He kept me alive. God had a plan. I just needed to seek Him for His plan for my life. I was trying, but I wasn't perfect in my endeavors.

It was the fall of 1989, when one of my friends and her husband decided to start a church. I could relate to them because they had been married once before and restored. They seemed like in the natural eye "used goods" too, so I felt comfortable with them. They asked me if I would help with the singles ministry. Of course, I did. I was just grateful to God that anybody would find something worthy in me. I knew I had a call on my life, but didn't know what to do with it. I was willing to do whatever to become someone worthy of the call. Jesus already made me worthy, but I didn't learn that for a very long time.

One night I received a phone call from the other singles leader, who had a child, too. She asked if I would call this gentleman with whom the pastor was trying to set her up. She wasn't interested in him at all. I said, "Of course, I will!" Remember, I didn't meet strangers, and if I did, they were my friends immediately. I could call and invite him to the next singles event; that was a piece of cake. So, I called this kind gentleman and invited him. He said he would try to make it.

That was the answer from most of the people I called. You know singles, committed to come unless some hot girl or guy called for a date. Been there done that. He couldn't see through the phone that I wasn't playboy material, neither did he know I was "used goods."

We started having weekly meetings at a local hotel on Thursday nights for the whole congregation. One of my greatest desires was to sing in a group. In my wild days, I always wanted to be in the "Go-Go's." They were an "all-girl band" that rocked! I wanted to rock and play the guitar. I'm sure to feed my flesh, not my spirit. All eyes would be on me.

They asked me to sing on the praise and worship team, and I felt like I had died and gone to heaven. I was honored. We would pray before service in the hallway after we practiced singing for the service. This night we were in the circle to pray when suddenly, this good-looking man came walking toward the door to go into church. The pastor said with his arms open, come join us. He did. I recognized his voice. He was the gentleman I called earlier in the week. I said, "You must be Rick Kramer." He smiled and said, "Yes, that's me." I just got nervous. He was a grown man, handsome at that. Who knew he was so hot? Not me, I didn't even know this guy. What I do remember is, after praying in the hallway, he took a seat right behind me.

What is so funny was I had a mole on the back of my head. I was afraid he would see it. I felt so self-conscious. I was afraid he wouldn't like me because he would see that stinking mole. I thought, *just add that to my used goods list. I'm used, not playboy material, and have a mole on the back of my head. Yep, that sounds really sexy doesn't it? Who's going to want someone like this?* I literally laugh out loud now, but at the time, it was once again my insecurities screaming out for love. My heart was saying, "please don't reject me due to my imperfections." Sad, but true; this was my truth.

All I could think about was Rick. I didn't want the service to end. I couldn't help but think about who was behind me and how cute he was and why the other singles director didn't want to be with him. After church, we began to talk. I discovered he was raising his two children alone—a boy named Ryan who was 13 and a precious little girl who was 11 named Lacey. I just couldn't imagine. That was so new for me to see a man step up like he had and take the responsibility of raising his two beautiful children, one a teenager at that. All I could think about was how I treated my mother during my rebellious years and the paybacks if I were to marry this man. Being a single parent is one of the hardest things to do. I understood, but I had only one child, how could he handle being the single parent of two? I was already crushing on him.

We talked for a few minutes after church, and we went our separate ways. I couldn't get this man off my mind. Brandon and I were still living with mom at the time, and I remember coming home telling her about this mysterious man. "Mom, he has two children, raising them alone, how courageous he must be."

Remember the guy I mentioned earlier, the one I met on a blind date? The one I would have sex with on a Saturday and cry out to Jesus for help on a Sunday? Let me try to describe him to you. He was a settled man that was very important to me. He worked out all the time so he was fit. That was important to me, too. He had never been married, and I was ok with that. How could I judge him if he was? He owned his own house on the lake, had a speedboat and a big dog named Bear. He was a family guy, and I loved that, yet his family was experiencing how to manage after being broken from divorce. I knew the feeling, just from a different perspective. I felt comfortable with him even though our belief systems were not the same. I felt I could adjust to anything, as long as he didn't cheat on me. I didn't think I was asking too much.

I trusted him. He didn't want to experience what his parents were going through. He was getting used to me having a child, but now, Brandon's dad would try to come see him more often. He could see my struggle when I had to learn how to share.

I didn't want to be alone, again, by myself. It was during this time, I met Rick. He started coming to the singles events and the other gentleman didn't have much to do with my church. He thought the people at my church were weird. He didn't think you should show emotion, or express yourself with lifting hands in church, much less have an interpretive dance team. Well, this little Pentecostal girl expressed herself wherever she went. If I decided to marry him, I would need to be ok with attending his local church, probably end up singing in the choir. But I wasn't a "choir robe" kind of girl. I was a "Go Go" wanna-be rock star, remember?

The singles ministry at my church, which I was co-leading, started doing activities most weekends. So, I found myself spending more time with Rick. I felt torn. I thought he was so cute and responsible. Where was my daddy when I needed him to help me make a good decision? I desperately wanted to take him home with me to see what kind of answer I would get from my daddy at the end of the table.

The singles group all agreed to go camping. Camping? Right! Just so you know, I don't camp; I'm not a happy camper. My style of camping is the Marriott or the Hilton. I like a shower without flip-flops. I went to church youth camps growing up, wearing flip-flops to avoid foot fungus and that just wasn't for me now in my life; but I went anyway. I was one of the ones in charge, so I had to be there. Obviously, it wasn't my idea. I didn't even own a sleeping bag. However, that night was Brandon's dad's weekend, so after the Mickey Mouse on Ice that I promised Brandon I would take him to, I took him to meet up with his dad. He stayed the weekend with him while I spent the night under the stars, freezing, but happy to be with people that I felt loved me, for me.

When I got to the campsite, my tent was up, the fire was going, and I was freezing. What in the world have I gotten myself into this time? My motive was to quickly find this guy, Rick Kramer. I could not stop thinking about him. You know, the real kind of man who was kind and sweet-spirited. He brought the children with him, but they were already asleep when I got there, plus they weren't interested in me at all. The next morning came bright and early, and by the end of the afternoon, we ended up playing volleyball. Bowling and volleyball were basically the only sports we could do in our denomination—at least that is what I thought. There was something different about this man. I just couldn't put my finger on it.

I had a list of what I wanted in a man this time around. I was trying to figure life, without daddy. My thoughts were: "WWDD, What Would Daddy Do?" I had dated some guys that I thought were cute, but they either had horrible breath or they were way too calm for this fireball. I felt like an average girl who was trying to learn how to live with Jesus and make a good living for her beautiful baby boy.

I wanted a man who, of course, loved God first. The next few things were so random; I don't know what I was thinking, but it's quite hilarious now. The second trait/quality was I wanted him to have dark hair. Why, I'm just not sure; must have been my personal preference. The third thing on my list was height. The fourth was to wear suits. The fifth was to play golf, and the sixth was to have a waterbed. Ok, stop laughing hysterically at me. I get it. The list is extremely shallow. I was kind of crazy back then, and I guess I still am, in some ways. The guy I was currently dating had only one of the things on my list; he loved God, his way, just not the way I was brought up. He still had five things left to fulfill my list of necessities in a man. God had a sense of humor when he created me. I'm sure I keep Him laughing.

I kept this list to myself. Thank God. I'm sure you are saying, "smart girl." I would look at the men I would date and see how they measured up to such "high standards." So far I hadn't met anyone to match my qualifications . . . until Rick Kramer. He loved God; he was tall, and dark-headed. Three out of the six . . . so far so good. The more I would hang out with him, the more I liked him. I was attracted to him. What I loved was his spirit; his heart was beautiful. So kind, giving, selfless; this kind of man was strange to me. So many character traits like my daddy. I thought if he could raise and nurture these two beautiful children, he surely could handle one more. And don't forget me, too. That shouldn't be too hard. But my heart was torn.

I had spent almost two years with this other guy I was currently dating, but he just couldn't commit to me. I didn't understand why. I just thought he was scared, because his parents had experienced divorce and he didn't want to raise a child that was not his flesh and blood. That always made me sad. But I would suppress my thoughts and believe that if he knew Brandon, he would fall more in love with him, too. It was hard, because he wouldn't see Brandon during the weekdays, just the weekends and sometimes every other weekend.

Lee College was having a basketball game. I loved to take Brandon to the games. I wanted him to have as much guy influence as he possibly could. Rick wanted to know if I was going to the game. He was attending Lee, but this time as a parent. He had attended years earlier, but recently decided to return to finish his degree.

Brandon and I decided to go to the game. As a protective mom, I tried to keep Brandon from most of my guy friends, at least until we were serious. I didn't want to confuse him this time, but Rick wasn't my boyfriend. I thought: *This friendship is harmless. We are just going to meet at a ballgame. Innocent? Right?* Wrong. Brandon was so young, only 5 years old at the time. He didn't know Rick or pay any attention to the guys from church. We got to the game, and Brandon was his usual self—happy, friendly, kind and generous, silly, full of energy, loving, and always looking out for his mommy. You never knew what would come out of Brandon's mouth. He would always come up with funny things to say.

To describe how funny Brandon was, one day I got a call from his day care. They said Brandon needed his lunch money. I said, "I give him lunch money every day." So, they asked Brandon where it was. His response was, he swallowed it; whatever his kindergarten classmates would dare him to do, he would do it. This day, it was to swallow his lunch money. Apparently, they dared him regularly. One of his teachers said, he must be saving up for his college education. The apple doesn't fall too far from the tree.

Back to the basketball game, I saw Brandon sitting by Rick. Reservedly, I was a bit concerned. I looked over and smiled with approval and corrective eyes, saying, "you better not get me in trouble." Then suddenly, Brandon yelled, in front of everyone, "Hey mom, this guy is single!" Yes, you got it; my face turned 50 shades of red! I was so embarrassed. That was and still is, Brandon. He always said what was on his mind. Those who know him love him for it. Some things never change. He is still that sweet young man now who speaks his mind and is protective of his mommy, always looking out for my best interest.

It was Christmastime. We had a play, and I invited my boyfriend to come and watch the play at the hotel. He was kind and generous to come to see me and be part of my world for an hour. Remember, he didn't care for the church; too charismatic, so I always felt torn. I had reserved two seats up front alongside my mom. Our pastors liked their leaders to sit up front. I am sure he felt nervous. He wasn't a "sit up front kind" of guy. Mom liked him. Ultimately, she just wanted me happy. She was still swallowed up in her own world of survival. She can't remember much about this season of my life . . . hers either. She was just trying to get through one day at a time. Trust me, I understood that feeling completely.

When my boyfriend finally got to the play, I walked him to the front and headed back to the back to greet the guests at the front door. I saw Rick there. He was running sound. He was intriguing, somewhat mysterious to me. There was something different about this "mysterious" man. I was curious about him. I knew I couldn't go further with my boyfriend of two years if I wanted to spend so much time with Rick. I was glad my boyfriend wasn't in a hurry to decide about marrying me now. Out of desperation, I probably would have married him. It would have been a bad decision.

Since I was trying to live for Jesus, raise my standards, and work on my reputation, I couldn't kiss two guys at the same time. I was working on my self-respect. I was extremely curious about what life would be like with Rick. After a few months of struggling between both men, it got the best of me. I broke up with my boyfriend of two years. He would beg me back. He finally wanted to commit and marry me. I cried myself to sleep many nights not knowing what to do. I felt he was just marrying me because he felt the pressure. I wanted someone to marry me because they loved me, for me. That scared me. He didn't. I would lie in bed at night asking God for a sign of what I was supposed to do. Was I making the right decision? Daddy where are you now? I needed help, direction, and wisdom. I couldn't trust my own emotions. I needed a sign. My heart was torn.

When my boyfriend finally bought the ring, I was devastated. This should have been a happy time in my life, but I felt like I was falling in love with Rick. Rick and I had so much more in common and he liked Brandon. Rick thought he was funny and appreciated his adventurous spirit. But I still felt unsure. Rick had just gone through a divorce and swore he would never get married again, until he met me. Why does he love me so much? Doesn't he get it? I'm "used goods!" I would go back and forth from Rick to my boyfriend. Until one night, I had decided to accept the ring from my now fiancé. He felt secure, steady. I needed steady; I needed security.

After my decision to accept the ring, I received a letter from Rick. He said the letter was written and inspired by the Holy Ghost. I had never heard that line before. Here was another divine letter. My daddy wrote me one, and now one from Rick. That's crazy, right? I thought, *God must love to write letters about me.* In the letter, he explained that if I married this other man, I would miss the will of God for my life. I got scared again. I had missed it so many times. I just wanted to truly do the right thing. I was learning what the will of God was for my life, but I was so confused.

While I had spent time with Rick, he began telling me his story of redemption. The more he talked about Jesus, the more I fell in love with him. He had been married 15 years in an unhealthy relationship and was adamant about not getting married. So, it was very surprising to read his letter, telling me if I married someone else, I would be making a huge mistake by not being his bride. Rick was fighting for me in this letter. I had never been fought for, except by my daddy. This was so unusual for me, but I loved it. He genuinely adored me, loved me with passion like Jesus.

Rick was 12 years older than I was. He had two teenagers. I was 26 years old with a boy 5 years of age. How in the world would this work? The portrait of my family growing up didn't look like this. But my heart was willing to take the chance, even though I felt like I was still a baby with milk around my own mouth. I chose Rick.

Used Goods

On June 2, 1990, I became Mrs. Rick(y) Glen Kramer, and I loved it. "Oh, God, please let his children love me too" was my prayer.

Self-Awareness: Have you ever been in love? Are you in love now? What does love look like to you? Are you settling for the good man because you don't want to be alone or do you have the courage to trust God and wait for the godly man Jesus Christ brings into your life? Perhaps you have standards you are compromising because of a personal lie. These are some of the questions to think about in internalizing where you are today. I never dreamed my life would be like it is today. I am happy, fulfilled, loved, but it hasn't always been this way because of my own personal lies.

Your Personal Lies: _____

_____

_____

_____

_____

_____

_____

_____

Your Personal Truths: _____

_____

_____

_____

_____

_____

Chapter 8

A New Tribe: The Kramers

I will never forget the day Rick and I got married. We didn't have any money. I had a little saved up, but I wasn't making a lot back then working as a sales representative for a travel agency. What I had was enough for two living at home with mom, but not five. My mom was still in her "insane days," as she calls it, and I didn't feel comfortable asking her for money to help with my wedding. Since I had married Brandon's daddy twice, I was now on my third marriage. I didn't see that one coming either. They say, three times is a charm. Well, for me it was. I married my prince charming.

Everything went great on the day of the wedding. It was very simple. We made a circle with all three children. Rick made a vow to Brandon, to love and cherish him as his own. I did the same to Ryan and Lacey. It was a beautiful ceremony, but I was still bruised from the wounds of my first husband and my dad's death. Whether through death or divorce, they both left me heartbroken. I told Rick, "I want to give you my whole heart, but I don't think I can." Rick was willing to take on the challenge of captivating my whole heart. I never, ever wanted to hurt that badly again. My guard was up; my walls were high.

Lacey wore a lace, miniature bride's dress. We laugh now, but she was miserable. My only other wish was to have my daddy walk me down the aisle. In my first marriage, my daddy told my husband, "I'm not giving my daughter away; I'm only letting you borrow her. If at any time, she needs to come back, I will always have her back." I took him up on that many times. In this case, marrying Rick was different. I believe if I could have had the opportunity to introduce him to my daddy at the dinner table, I would have received a headshake of approval. "Yes, marry this man. Don't let this one go."

After the wedding reception, we were getting ready to leave for our honeymoon and Brandon started bawling, tugging on my dress. I was going to be away from him for a week. We had never been away from each other that long. I hated to see him cry. He was so young. He didn't understand what divorce meant. All he knew was his parents weren't living together, and he was traveling back and forth on weekends. Now, he had to share me with another man. Life didn't seem fair, I'm sure. And it wasn't.

All the odds, according to society, were against us. Blending two families together isn't easy. The divorce ratio is higher after your first marriage. I was so young, and all I knew was Rick was a survivor like me. We could make it through "hell or high water."

These difficulties were quickly tested after we came home from the honeymoon. Our new reality got real, quickly. So young and unlearned, I was trying to figure out and understand how blended families were supposed to work and be successful. I wanted to be Ryan and Lacey's super hero. *I know I can make all their hurts heal, with my love for them,* I thought. What I soon realized was Rick fell in love with me, but the children didn't. I was the outsider taking the place of their mom . . . in their eyes. They weren't happy about it. They were dealing with their feelings of hurt, pain, rejection, and abandonment, too. I understand it was a bit awkward. I was 12 years younger than Rick. The age difference between Rick and me never bothered me. Somehow, I always thought I would marry an older man. I was fine with it.

I didn't understand how awkward it was until I went to one of Rick's college reunions. They all knew his first wife. Some of his friends didn't keep close touch with him, and they had no idea he was divorced. Then suddenly, he would introduce me. For all they knew, he left her for me. I wanted to put a note on my back that said, "I am not a home wrecker." When they got to know me, they liked me.

My prayer was that Ryan and Lacey would learn to love me back. You can't force love, but embracing them with love will. What I have learned about raising children is, you must make room in your plan to allow your children to make decisions on their own. If they fail at their plan, love them anyway. Failure isn't a person; it's an event. If they don't succeed at their plan, love them anyway. Take time to get to know what they love. When we first got married, I made so many mistakes. I wanted the children to be structured, make their bed, clean their rooms, put their dishes in the sink, and please don't eat all the cereal. I wanted a bowl, too, especially Captain Crunch with crunch berries or Lucky Charms. It is funny now, but I wasn't used to sharing. I don't share well. Who knew I would have to learn to share my cereal! (Ok, I will be honest. I would sometimes hide the Lucky Charms for myself. Selfish, I know.)

To make life more exciting, one day I came home from a long day at work. The children would come home from school only to be left home alone. That's the best we could do. Ryan was 13. He could watch Lacey and Brandon. However, they were clever. They put their minds together and thought, Let's forget about homework. It would be really cool to make the living room into a fort. The couch was turned over; the lounge chair was flipped over, and the kids were sliding down the stairs on their pillows. I was so frustrated, because the house was a disaster. It is funny now, but back then, I wasn't used to that kind of chaos. I was raised if you went to spend the night at your friend's house you had to be home by 10 a.m. the next morning to do your chores. My chaos was different. I had to quickly adjust or my life was going to be extremely frustrating. I had to seek counseling on how to handle my new normal.

I was in the shower one morning, overwhelmed from life, and crying and thinking, What in the world have I done? I am a baby, 26 years old, with milk around my mouth trying to raise two teenagers. God help me be a better me, a better wife, a better mom. And since I know God's voice when He speaks to me, I listened as He assured me, He had equipped me for this journey. He said, "You can't heal what is broken, but you can help restore what was stolen."

I love my two older children like they came from my womb. I would do anything in this world for them. We have grown into a beautiful family, and I attribute all the success to God. He has and will always be the center of our family circle. We couldn't make it without God's wisdom and direction in our lives. When God restores something, He doesn't restore it to its original state, but greater. I had to learn that I wasn't super woman. I needed to retire the super-woman cape. If I didn't, I was going to crash and burn quickly and not rescue anyone. I am a fixer, and I wanted to fix their lives on my terms, not theirs. I have apologized to my children since then for not having all the answers about the right way to live in a blended family. They so graciously have accepted my apology. We had to grow in love. I am glad to say that today they love me back.

Not only were we all adjusting to having a blended family, but also Rick and I were adjusting to being newlyweds. This was new to both of us. I was raised to always do your best. Always. My daddy taught me I could do anything. I had to continually tell myself that.

One day Rick came home and I noticed there was no vehicle in the driveway. Much to my surprise, they had repossessed his car that morning. He proceeded to tell me he had missed a few payments that he promised we would pay back to his friend. Although Rick understood his friend's position, he was still without a vehicle. He was afraid of how I would respond. We either feed the children or drive the car. I felt so badly for him. He was trying so hard to provide for his new blended family. I knew he felt like a failure. I never saw Rick through the eyes of a failure. He was a hard worker. I saw deep down inside the man God designed him to be. He was a work in progress, too, like me. I would do anything for and was very much in love with this God-fearing, selfless man. Although I kept pieces of my heart to myself, my walls were slowly coming down, one brick at a time. I would always try to treat people the way I wanted to be treated. Words of condemnation and criticism would only hurt him even more and make things worse, so I would just keep encouraging him, cheering him on, regardless of the situations we faced. Praise is better than persecution. I just kept praising, praying, and asking God to help us.

All this change transpired within the first four months of our marriage. The next few months got increasingly worse. He lost another job because of downsizing. We found ourselves living off my income of only little more than $17,000 a year. Times were troubled.

I was a giver and Rick embraced that same principle. God became real to him while he was learning the parable of reaping and sowing. We saw how God was providing for us right before our eyes. We never stopped giving. God was our provider. We were learning it was all His in the first place. God is the one who gives us the ability to get wealth. We would always try to help others. We were getting a little more in our checking account.

Rick heard about this young man needing a car in our church. He had drug abuse in his background, and Rick was trying to show him the heart of Jesus. Rick felt compassion for this young man and gave him his car. Rick knew what it was like to walk down that path of drug abuse. Rick was to him, Jesus with skin on. It was by no means a Cadillac, but it was better than the guy walking from place to place. At least he could have transportation to get to work. This was one more confirmation of why I fell in love with Rick; his heart was so kind and generous.

It wasn't long after he was let go from one job that he was hired at another place. The owners were friends of my parents when we lived in Europe. We were excited, because we just knew this was going to be a great career move for him—something he could do for a long time. We felt settled, for a minute. Rick worked in the insurance business for years, so he had knowledge in this field; whereas, the owner of the company didn't. So, when the owner asked him to head up another division in this industry, Rick thought it was great. He was already knowledgeable in this field, and he was excited. He would come from work and talk about his experiences. I would try to relate and get excited with him in his world. He excelled. He presented a proposal for a new account and they loved it. It brought great revenue into the owner's company. What it also showed to the owner was Rick was a genius in this field and was much smarter than she was. Jealousy isn't attractive. In fact, it's quite ugly.

Right before Christmas 1990, Rick went to work like any ordinary day. The owner of the company asked to see him in her office. His thoughts were that she was thinking he had done such a great job; she might want to talk about raising his salary. She proceeded to let him know she needed his keys to the office, and his beeper, only to be handed his pink slip. "You're fired," she said. Startled would be an understatement. Rick was devastated. Grasping for words from being completely shocked, his first response was, "please, tell me, what I have done so badly that would warrant you firing me?" He proceeded to validate his work ethic, pleading his case. "I thought you loved the proposal; we got the account. I brought in more revenue than you were making. I took this industry to another level, added another division, and I'm fired?" I will do whatever you want, whatever you need. You don't understand I have a brand-new family to provide for. Please give me another chance, what can I do?" She responded, "you can beg for it." Humbly, Rick began begging for his job back. She laughed and handed him his pink slip.

Oh, God, what am I going to tell Sandi, was going through his mind. In the first six months of our marriage, Rick lost two jobs, one car, and had to file bankruptcy due to medical bills from his previous marriage. Graciously, we were learning together how to live in this new tribe called The Kramers.

Self-Awareness: What an interesting time in my life. You may have had a few years like mine. You wonder, is this what life is all about? Am I ever going to succeed at anything? How do I know how to blend this family? I remember thinking: *If this roller coaster of life doesn't stop and let me off, I'm going to literally jump off this ride, and try sky diving.*

My personal lies were going crazy. Failure tried to invade my head again in my life, and I had to cope with knowing God would not fail me. I knew He said, He would be with me and would equip me for this journey, but I couldn't see the light at end of this dark long tunnel.   Now it's your turn. Write down your personal lie and overcome it with three personal truths.

Your Personal Lies: _____

_____

_____

_____

_____

_____

_____

_____

Your Personal Truths: _____

_____

_____

_____

_____

_____

_____

Lies, Liar, and the Lioness

Chapter 9

Tragedy to Triumph

If you look at the word, "triumph" the word consists of "tri" and "umph." Rick's *umph* was exhausted. He was trying and trying to make something happen for his new family and nothing seemed to work. He was mentally and physically overwhelmed with so much stuff that he found himself lying on the couch swallowed up in depression.

Why would a so-called "Christian woman" do this to me? Rick thought. *How ruthless.* I would come home from work, a type "A" personality, only to find him lying on the couch, lifeless, with no vision. I would try to encourage him. I prayed over him continually, but the truth was we both knew Christmas was quickly approaching. He didn't want to disappoint his new wife and child, much less his own children. Until one day, something amazing happened while he was lying on the couch. Rick had a GM: A "God Moment." A GM is when, like Joshua, God stops time and begins to invade your space with His ways and purpose. God begins to transcend one's thoughts and ideas so much that you aren't the same after the encounter.

Let me try to explain it. I walked in the house from work and Rick said, "Babe, I have just had an amazing thought, and I honestly believe it is from God—a God Moment. Well, I loved this now because when I left him earlier, he was depressed and defeated; now I've come home and he's energized and full of life. His spiritual vision had returned. And if you know anything about me, you know I don't do depression well or negativity, so for me to come home to a happy man was amazing. He proceeded to tell me that the Lord told him:

"Since you had the tools to create the job for her, you can use these same tools to create a job for your family. And the Lord said to call it, 'Tennessee Temps.'"

So many times, I have heard the saying, "When God closes one door, He opens up another one." Please let me encourage you. If God has closed one door in your life, He will open another. If God started it, He will complete it! I try to always look at the positives in life. If his former boss had not fired him, then he might still be employed by someone else. Instead, God knew He could trust Rick Kramer to enlarge his mindset and open new possibilities. I don't know who is reading this book, but let me encourage you. When God closes one door and it looks bleak, dim, and dreary and you are afraid, Father says to you this day to "Fear not and don't be afraid." God will give you the strength, wisdom, peace, and funds to walk out the purpose and the plan.

When Rick had his "God Moment," God didn't tell him the whole plan. Rick had to continue to seek Him with the blueprints of the plan for this new adventure he was about to enter. Noah had a similar situation; he had to listen for the architectural design for the ark to save the people from the Flood. Rick had to listen to save our family from financial destruction. God will not lead you in one direction without giving you a plan. He may only instruct you step-by-step, because if He told you the whole idea you wouldn't trust in Him any longer. You would become dependent upon yourself rather than staying focused on God. God delights in His children, trusting and listening to His voice daily in their lives. God knows what you need before you even ask.

People will always disappoint you. Tell them thank you for making you stronger. Stop right now and take a moment to say thank you for the relationships Jesus spared you from in your life. For all the men that rejected me: "Thank you." For all the people who said I wouldn't amount to anything: "Thank you." For the people who would never give me a chance because I was used goods: "Thank you." Now, I can look back in retrospect and appreciate the rejection, the lack of acceptance, and the unbelief that I would become something, because I am something, because God is something. I am nothing without Him.

Rick got up from the couch that day with excitement, and the direction he felt was best for this blended family. I trusted him and believed in him. If he said he heard from God, he indeed did. He then called a family meeting with his dad and my mom. With Jesus as the CEO, $600.00 and a friend who believed in him, Rick started Tennessee Temps, Inc., January 16, 1991. So please be encouraged when it looks dark and you are desperate for an intervention, be open for a "God Moment." It will change your life forever.

I continued to work at the travel agency and helped Rick at night if he needed me. We became a team. Trust was our foundation along with God being the silent listener to every conversation. We grew together in life, love, and with God. But the business became stagnant. We needed to go to a higher level. Rick wasn't drawing much of a paycheck. We wanted to grow the business, but it was during a recession in 1992.

We continued to give, but the business remained the same. One night our pastor invited a popular singing group to sing at our church where we were serving at the time. Rick was an elder, and I was leading worship occasionally for the main congregation, but primarily working closely with the Women's Ministry. We loved our church. We loved being involved in whatever God was involved in, and it seemed like He pitched His tent amid this congregation. On this night, the leader of the singing group took up an offering. I felt in my heart and spirit what we were to give. Rick looked at me; at the same time, I looked at him. Believe it or not, he confirmed the same amount I had in my heart. We were to give it all! Since Rick saw how I handled the money being single with Brandon, I took care of the finances in our household. Unaware of the amounts, he asked what we had in our savings and what we had in our checking account. I told him the amount. We wrote out a check for what was left in our checking accounts—all but $2.37.

We knew we were to give it all away. We both are givers; however, sometimes I can get a bit carried away. Rick is a big giver, too, but he is much more balanced than I am. That is just one of the many characteristics he has taught me over the years. He always tried to describe me as a "consistent extremist." That I was. So for us to agree on the same idea or amount had to be God. Giving all we had with three children, one being a young teenage boy who would eat everything (I mean everything) seemed crazy. But we wanted to be obedient. By faith, we wrote the check and named our seed. We waited, and waited, and waited, for almost 90 days.

Silence. Nothing seemed to happen in the business until the eleventh hour. Suddenly, months later, after writing the check and emptying our bank accounts, we landed a new account that set us on the map. Increase was the seed, and increase is what we received. We were spellbound and shocked. We knew God could do it, but we were still astonished at His generosity. He is a faithful God. We had seen Him move mountains on many occasions. We were extremely thankful for His faithfulness to our family.

And the good news is, the business is still flourishing. We are so grateful, and thankful to God. We consider ourselves honored that God would entrust something so special to us as this business. We are merely stewards. He has always been our CEO.

What was formerly known as Tennessee Temps, was changed to iKruit Staffing in 2011. We celebrated 25 years in 2016. After 25 years of working hard, our motto on our sign says, "Work hard or go home." Even when you can't see him working, He is working the night shift.

Self-Awareness: Sometimes to get to the next level in life you must give something up that is of value to you to show your dependence isn't on you, but that you truly trust God and his provision for your life. Look at your current situation. Is there something that you could or should give up to God to show you are serious about trusting him first, above all else? Or perhaps you feel like you can "do life" without God's help. Trust God. There is something God can't do, and that is fail. His Word is true, and He will never fail you.

Your Personal Lies: _____

_____

_____

_____

_____

_____

_____

_____

Your Personal Truths: _____

_____

_____

_____

_____

_____

_____

Chapter 10

Surprise

I love surprises. God ones. Rick and I had been married for three years. Tennessee Temps had been in business for 2 ½ years. God had miraculously intervened and the business was growing. I was still working part-time until we were surprised by a blessing. Rick was now 42, and I had just turned 30. Brandon was 10, in elementary school; Lacey was 15, and experiencing high school life. Ryan was 17 years old, living in North Carolina. Our lives were full, experiencing all the wonders of blending families, both happy times and tough ones. We decided it was a mutual decision for the both of us to just be content with the family members we already had. We both were growing older and our finances were already stretched. Adding an addition to this family would be crazy. But what did we know? Absolutely nothing.

We decided for me to get my tubes tied in June of 1992. But, God had a greater plan and purpose for this blended family. Waking up every morning feeling nauseated wasn't a very good sign. So being familiar with the feeling of being pregnant, I went to the doctor only to confirm our suspicious minds, we were having a baby. Morning sickness became my morning friend; or should I say my morning enemy. I was never sick past the first trimester of being pregnant with Brandon, but this little surprise blessing was different. I was sick the entire pregnancy . . . all day, every day. This caused me to be released from my job and help Rick at Tennessee Temps as much as I could.

I remember clearly going into Rick's office after the doctor's appointment confirming, we were pregnant. He was shocked. We both were surprised. It took his breath away. He sat down in the chair, gasping with words of encouragement, knowing God must have a greater plan. We will get through this. One more hurdle for us because of our age, even after already going through so much together. What was next for us, we never saw coming.

Since I had already had a boy, my heart was leaning toward having a little girl. I could dress her up like a baby doll. Since I got Lacey at 11, she wasn't too fond of my dressing her up like a princess. She has always had an independent, strong-willed spirit, and that is just one of the many things I love about her. Her will caused her to survive all the opposition and trials she endured during the years before I was blessed to have her in my life. How great it would be for her to have a sister. I had never birthed a little girl, so my heart's desire was for Lacey to have a playmate. Although she was 15, I doubt that was her thought. Lacey was thinking more like a babysitter . . . free at that.

When I went in for the ultra sound to determine the due date of the baby and gender, much to my surprise, they said my baby was a boy. No way; it couldn't be a boy. You don't understand, I felt like I had heard from God.

Let me explain. One night lying in my bed I woke up at midnight from a deep sleep. I nudged Rick from his sleep only to tell him, "I believe I know what we are to name the baby. And it's a girl. I believe her name is Rachel Nicole Kramer." Come to find out, Rachel means, Lamb of God. "That's it, Babe, we will call her Rachel Nicole, and Rachel Nicole she will be." I bought all kinds of girlie things, pink colors of course. So, when I went to the doctor, he surprised me when he saw a turtle. I was shocked. No way! It can't be! I still believed my doctor missed it, because I was confident I had heard from God.

It was November of 1992; Ryan had flown home to be with us for Thanksgiving. I was honored to sing in the praise and worship team at our church. Rick decided he would take Brandon with him early to the airport, while I would bring Lacey with me when the service was over.

This beautiful surprise baby was always settling on my main artery that gives oxygen to the brain. When that flow gets shut off or cut off from flowing properly, it would cause me to faint. Well, I had been to the doctor a few times because of this, and she said it was an anxiety attack, I needed to just calm down. Her advice for me was to look out the window and count the cars to get my mind off the anxiety.

Knowing the person that I am, that was ridiculous advice! There was no way that was me. After all I had been through in life previously, and not on any medicine, counting cars was simply ridiculous, much less my having an anxiety attack. She obviously didn't know me. She didn't get me. I could handle any obstacle set before me, especially without counting the cars! Well, this day happened to be one of those days the baby was on my artery.

After saying our goodbyes to Ryan, Rick and Brandon went in one car and Lacey and I went in my car. It was a red sports car and not much room. Heading back from Chattanooga to Cleveland, suddenly, I said to Lacey, "Babe, Mom can't see. The baby is on my artery again, and I feel like I'm about to pass out. You're going to have to tell me how fast I'm driving and if I am staying on the road." We were on I-75 with traffic in all directions. I said, "Lacey if you know how to pray, in the Spirit, you need to pray now." She was so precious I began to hear her praying. After 20 minutes of her telling me how to drive, between praying, she said, "Mom, if you don't slow down you're going to hit the car in front of us." I pulled the car to the right so far it sent us off the road, through a sign, and into a ditch, heading for a large area of mucky water. Suddenly, the car stopped; I passed out at the wheel.

Rick was in front of us, because we were following behind. He pulled over off the highway, came over to where I was, opened my side of the door, and I fell half way out of the car, unconscious. Rick remembers Brandon saying, "Is she dead?" Rick didn't know what had happened to me, but he had seen me like this before because of all the episodes he had witnessed for himself.

Suddenly, across the highway was an ambulance. We didn't call it; divinely, it just showed up. The ambulance driver saw the accident and crossed over the median to where we were. They put me into the ambulance, and off I went to the hospital only to find when I got there, my pregnancy chart was wrong. The same doctor who told me to count the cars to relieve my anxiety had written down my dates wrong.

I was completely unconscious the whole time all this was transpiring. So when I got to the hospital, I miraculously awoke, only to hear the doctors saying, "We are going to have to take the baby. The baby is in trauma." They looked at my chart, and I heard them say, "She's 36 weeks." I sat up from the unconscious state of mind I was in and said to the doctors, "No I am not, I am only 32 weeks." So after putting the monitor on me to make sure the baby's vitals were still good, they rushed me to a hospital 45 minutes away. That hospital was capable of taking better care of me, and my traumatized baby.

I would come in and out of consciousness. I woke up in a very dark room. I felt extremely hot inside. It felt like my body was on fire. I'm thought to myself, *Surely I didn't die and go to hell? I thought I was doing pretty good.* I know that sounds funny, but that is what I thought. Suddenly, I woke up to see Rick in this dark room. He was sitting there praying for me. When I looked at him, he was so happy I had opened my eyes. Oh, how our lives would be different if I had not made it through this trying time. I was so happy to see him. I asked him what was going on. I had no idea where I was. When I began to tell him I felt hot, he told me they put this medicine directly in my veins to stop me from giving birth to our baby. I was having contractions; I was in labor.

The doctor told me about the trauma the two of us endured. But all I could think about was how grateful I was to be alive, and my baby, too. He continued to explain that I must carry the baby for another four weeks at least because "he" only weighed 3 lbs. I said, "We are having a girl!" The doctor said, the ultra sound picture says you are having a boy. Sure, enough, we were having a boy! He saw the turtle, too.

Ok, I missed God's voice, again. It wasn't the first time, and it won't be the last, I'm sure. I am so glad Old Testament customs aren't practiced today, or I would have stone marks all over my body from being a false prophet. I could have sworn we were having a girl. After getting over the realization I had been adamantly wrong about the gender of our child, my immediate focus went to praying for a healthy, baby boy.

The day arrived, and I was informed I would need to have a caesarean. They scheduled the surgery and the delivery of our beautiful surprise baby boy. After being high risk for almost three months, and visiting the doctor every week, on February 4, 1993, our beautiful baby boy was born, weighing 8 lbs. 8 oz., and he was 19 inches long. Rick was taking selfies before selfies were even cool. Proud

Dad. I felt like my stomach was being torn apart from the doctor pulling the baby out so hard. I could not see the process of the birth, but Rick could. All I could do was feel the pressure. After the last pull, I felt the emptiness in my belly. I knew he was born. But my baby wasn't crying. I asked Rick, "Why isn't he crying, please talk to me." Silence filled the room. Rick hesitated to tell me. After all we had been through, our sweet baby was born blue. They took him from my womb and immediately placed him under a lamp pushing on his fragile chest trying to make his lungs respond. He couldn't breathe. Suddenly, I heard a cry, a little wimpy cry. That beautiful sound was music to our ears. The room filled with joy.

Since I was truly convinced we were having a baby girl, and we knew her name, we didn't discuss boy names. One day I was watching a Christian program, and I heard her say the meaning of Jordan. Jordan means crossing over to the fulfillment of God's promises. We had never thought of that as a name, but when I heard what it meant, I was confident that would be our baby's name. He had crossed over from death to life already, so we knew Father's promises were already being fulfilled in his life.

He was born with a little red birthmark on his forehead. It looked like lip prints. I always thought my daddy had kissed him first then sent him to be part of our blended family. After Rick saw his face he said, "His name must be King." He is a conqueror. He will overcome any situation and rule. So, we named him after my daddy—Roy Edwin King. And trust me; he ruled the house like a king. Seriously. No joke.

The devil is a liar. The Bible tells us that the Enemy of our soul wants to steal, kill, and destroy our lives. It is interesting because the Enemy tried to kill both of my seeds—Brandon from abortion and King from a car wreck.

Self-Awareness: What is it that the Enemy of your soul is trying to steal, kill, and destroy in your life? Perhaps you are facing devastating opposition right now and you feel like everything around you is dying. Have you had something stolen from you or destroyed right before your eyes? You can do something about it. You can surrender. Surrender your life from your control and allow Jesus to control your destiny from this day forward. When you begin to relinquish control over your present circumstances you cannot change, you will see a divine intervention in your life. Today is the day for God to breathe into you new life. But first, you must stop believing the Enemy's lies that you will not make it and your life is over.

YourPersonalLies:_____

_____

_____

_____

_____

_____

_____

Your Personal Truths: _____

_____

_____

_____

_____

_____

Chapter 11

Blind Faith

I have a generational curse in my family's DNA. You ask, "What in the world is a generational curse?" It is something that has been passed down from generation to generation. It is biblical. It is transferred from my gene, my bloodline. I understand the generational curse, because it is passed down from my gene into my boys. It is an eye disorder called, ocular albinism. It means the eyes have no pigmentation in the retinas. Like Albinos have no pigmentation in their skin, ocular albinism means no pigmentation in the retinas.

I didn't know much about this disease because I am a girl, and it is passed down to the male gender. However, the female gender carries the gene. Because my nephew was my sister's firstborn boy, he struggled with this eye disorder as well. When I found out I was pregnant with a son, I knew my child would battle this eye disorder. That devastated me for him. Earlier in my life, watching Brandon struggle and walking this journey with him, I bore the guilt even though it wasn't my sin that caused it for him. I hated to see him struggle, and I knew it came directly from my genes.

When I was deciding whether to abort Brandon, I felt the emotion of depression. I never embraced that emotion because I have a survival instinct. Even when I was struggling with the obstacles of an eating disorder, two failed marriages, and having a child before marriage, depression/suicide wasn't my continual battle. I always tried to see the best in every situation, but sometimes the situation got the best of me. This time, the fight wasn't about my bad decisions or me; it was my Brandon.

He was getting ready for kindergarten, and I had to take him to the eye doctor. I had to face the fact that this eye disease, as much as I prayed and prayed, went through healing lines with him, and anointed him with oil, still wasn't healed. I knew God had the power to heal him, but for some reason, God was choosing not to. As a parent, I couldn't grasp that concept. I had just watched God choose to take my earthly father home, and now I was in a faith battle over Brandon's eyesight.

When I took Brandon to the eye doctor, the doctor proceeded to tell me that they were going to fit him with very thick glasses and to top it off, jeweler lenses on the top of the glasses. The doctor thought it would be in his best interest that he could move the magnifying glass attached to the eyeglasses for reading something up close. I was devastated. My anger toward God was intensifying.

One day while I was working in Chattanooga as a sales representative for a travel agency, I was walking from the parking lot to the street where the agency was located. Walking on the sidewalk was this blind person with a seeing-eye dog, helping him navigate his way. I was so upset with watching Brandon struggle with this eye disorder, and honestly, I was frustrated with God. I knew He could heal him, but He wasn't listening, so I thought. When I got out of my car, I heard my inner voice telling me to go pray for the blind person. All I could think about was that big dog biting me as I approached him. My conversation with God kind of went like this: *Don't you see that big dog? Are you sure you want me to just walk up behind him? I'm a stranger, and that dog is huge.* Immediately I heard, *Just be obedient. I will take care of the rest.* So, I did. I gently walked up behind the blind person. I said, "Excuse me, please; I am not here to hurt you. I just want to pray for you. Is that ok?" The blind man, turned around, while the big dog was sniffing my leg. I thought the dog was either going to pee on me or bite me. Thank goodness neither happened. The dog backed off, and I continued the assignment I felt I was to do. I was trying to walk in obedience. I asked, "Do you know Jesus?" He so sweetly, nodded his head, yes. I proceeded to express my belief in healing and told him I would like to pray for his eyes. I did. I was elated. I got to pray for someone else who was going through what my child was going through. I began to cry while walking down the street. I turned around to see if the blind man was still safe on the street. He was gone. I couldn't believe it. Where did he go so quickly? Hebrews 13:2 immediately came to mind: "Do not forget to show hospitality to strangers, for by so doing some people have shown hospitality to angels without knowing it." He was an angel. Jesus was testing my heart of obedience. I passed the test. The feeling of satisfaction was overwhelming.

Brandon was such a cute, loving, kind, fun-filled, and easy-going child, but when the doctor showed him what the glasses looked like, he was devastated, too. I could see it on his little face. Fighting back the tears going home from the doctor's office, I was grasping for words to encourage him. All I could think about was other children making fun of him, bullying him, hurting him with words that would crush his spirit. My heart was sick and my hope was deferred. I came home from that doctor's appointment depressed for him, because I felt like I had caused this tragedy. My genes had caused this mess, along with all the other challenges and guilt that goes along with not being married to his dad.

I remember lying in bed, crying for at least two days straight. Rick had never seen me like this before. I was always the cheerleader, encourager, and motivator. Now I needed someone to encourage me. I needed a stranger, or an angel to pray for me.

Days later I was praying and crying in the shower. A still small voice whispered to me that He loved Brandon more than I did, and He was going to take care of him. Everything was going to be all right. I hadn't heard those words in years. The only one who ever said that to me was my earthly daddy and now my heavenly Father was encouraging me with a phrase that He alone knew I would understand. I cherish those moments when all the obstacles, challenges, and opposition, which look unbeatable and unmovable, start fading away when an encouraging word that gives hope comes to you. Jesus was praying for me. He is my intercessor.

That is just what I did. I knew God would take care of Brandon regardless of what we were to face in the days to come. We didn't put those new glasses on Brandon. When he was six, we did buy him glasses, but they were without the jeweler magnifying attachment. He was a cutie. All the girls loved him, and everything was all right with the world for a moment.

Here I was, now with another little baby boy. Oh, Jesus, please spare King from this generational curse, was my prayer. King was six-weeks old when I took him for a regular routine checkup. The doctor entered the room and asked me to lay King down on the table. I gently laid him down. She picked up the light to check his eyes. My fears were screaming inside of me; however, the room was silent. His pediatrician moved the light back and forth from side to side and King didn't follow the light. I was thinking, *Come on baby King, follow the light, please Jesus, please.* She was quiet, trying several times to get his attention. Because of what she had to tell me, she asked me to wrap him up and sit down. I wrapped him tightly in his favorite, warm blanket. The room felt cold. I felt alone and scared. Her tone of voice caused my heart to feel sorrowful. I knew what was coming next. My heartbeat accelerated from the news. She started writing in his chart with her head down. She took her pen and put it in her pocket, turned slowly and looked at me with compassion in her eyes. What she proceeded to tell me was my truth. I was going to have to face another one of my worst fears. My fears were glaring at me, mocking me in the face of defeat.

I knew if I had a girl, I would never have to face this eye disorder again. I honestly did not want to bring another child into this world to endure the opposition I saw Brandon struggle through. He hated the word, "special." He was in a school classroom of "special-needs" children; yet on the outside he looked completely normal. You could never tell any difference from his outward appearance. It was affecting him on the inside.

Fighting back the tears, I already knew what she was going to say. I heard the words, "Mrs. Kramer, King isn't following the light." "I am so very sorry to tell you this, but I am going to send you to a geneticist. I'm 99 percent sure your son is blind. His eyes aren't responding at all." With a few minutes of silence and for a moment for me to catch my breath in facing the reality of my fear, she said, "I am going to leave the room. This will give you a few moments, alone with him while I make the arrangements for you to see the specialist."

The doctor graciously left the room. I pulled King into my chest and begin to declare the words of Jesus over him. "King Kramer you will walk in healing in Jesus name. This disease will not conquer you. You will conquer it." Professing my faith loudly, adamantly, and with the authority I knew only Jesus could provide, I paced back and forth in that doctor's room. I declared, "My Father's Word tells me that if I decree a thing it shall be established; therefore, I am decreeing this doctor's report is wrong. My baby will see. He will not be blind."

The doctor entered the room and gave me the instructions to see the specialist in two weeks. I asked her to please tell me what I need to be looking for in receiving my miracle. Her response was, "If he watches you walk from one side of the room to the other."

I said, "Doctor, I will bring him back, and you will see my miracle baby."

I came home from the doctor's office thinking about how I was going to tell Rick. Guilt and shame tried to captivate my heart again with accusing words that this was my fault. I have caused this baby sorrow in life. My faith was failing quickly from my own thoughts. I had to rehearse the words of my heavenly Father again, over and over: "My grace is sufficient for you."

Recently, I was led to do a study on Mephibosheth from the Book of 2 Samuel 9. Cool story. What I learned brought me consolation. My hope is that it will encourage you as well.

Mephibosheth was Jonathan's son. Jonathan was King Saul's son, so Mephibosheth was King Saul's grandson. Jonathan and David were "bros."

King David asked, "Is there anyone still left of the house of Saul to whom I can show kindness for Jonathan's sake?" Jonathan unfortunately was killed in the battle. The story continues that David summoned one of Saul's servants and asked this question again. The servant said, "Yes, Mephibosheth, Jonathan's son, is in exile in Lo Debar."

The crazy cool part of this story is how Mephibosheth wound up in Lo Debar. He was in exile because the enemy was headed to his house. The Scripture references his age at about 5 years old. His caretaker picked him up, but while running from the enemy, she dropped him, and he became crippled in both legs. You say, "That's not very cool." You're right; it's not. But what is cool is years later God reminded David of his best friend Jonathan and his faithfulness to him and instructs him to go to his region to bless anyone left in his lineage. Jonathan, once again, is Mephibosheth's daddy. David doesn't know what happened to Mephibosheth or where he is or why he is hiding. God just wanted David to find someone in Jonathan's lineage to bless.

Imagine being Mephibosheth. You can't walk because someone who was supposed to protect you and watch over you dropped you. Does that sound familiar? Has anyone ever "dropped" you? Disappointed you? Someone to whom you were entrusted, perhaps a parent who decided to choose drugs over you, or maybe the person who was to shield you from danger instead placed you in danger and you were molested by your relative? Or, even a member in your church?

When studying this story, I heard in the voice I know to be my Savior's, without condemnation say, *You feel like you dropped Brandon and King because it's your DNA that caused their eye disorder.* It was true. For years, I carried the guilt, just like Mephibosheth's caretaker. I was responsible for the pain my boys were experiencing because of my DNA. The great relief of my story is my boys don't blame me. They both know, if I could heal them I would, or if somehow I could carry this cross for them, I would. Jesus was beaten beyond recognition for this disease; therefore, I didn't have to carry it. I just have to trust that Jesus knows best. I felt peace in trusting and knowing; my heavenly Father knows best. If you feel like you've been dropped, Jesus is right there to pick you up and carry you to His table where you belong.

Two weeks were a very long time to wonder if your child could see you smile. While rocking King to sleep, I would hear Rick crying and praying over him, declaring the words of the Lord, "By your stripes Jesus, King is healed." Finally, the two weeks came. We took King to the geneticist to draw the blood to see what we were up against with his eyes. I explained what I knew about ocular albinism and told her of our family history.

The report came back that with this eye disorder there is a 50/50 chance that the second-born baby would have the same disorder. She confirmed King did. A few weeks later, I was working in our bedroom walking from side to side when I saw King's sweet little head turn, following me from one side of the room to the other. I could not contain my excitement. I was a witness to the miracle right before my eyes. I took him back to the doctor to show her the great progress King made. We received our miracle. We danced our happy dance in the doctor's office. I thought, *Now whose laughing devil? You thought you would get the best of us, but you didn't. We win. Always, when you have Jesus, you win.*

Brandon and King are very close. Not only do they share the same disability, the eye disorder, but they also understand one another and what obstacles in life they would face. To this day, it truly is unbelievable how they cope in life. Do I believe God can heal them both completely? Absolutely, the answer is yes, without a doubt in my mind. Do I wish I could take it from them? Absolutely, the answer is yes, with no doubt in my mind. Do I believe God has a plan and I trust His timing in their healing? Absolutely, the answer is yes, with no doubt in my mind. I trust Jesus even when I can't see. It's called blind faith.

Self-Awareness: Life is unfair. I so desperately wish I could take from my boys their eye disorder. I watched both the boys' struggles and pray every day that God completes what he has started in them. I have faith to believe that God will, but until he does, I continue to have faith to believe. What have you believed God for, for so long but have yet to see the completion? Perhaps you are in God's waiting room, waiting for a miracle in your marriage, or for the salvation of your children, or maybe a physical healing in your own body. Yet, the Enemy keeps telling you it will never happen. The lie is bigger to you than your truth. I completely understand. Please may I encourage you to never give up, but keep believing, regardless of what you see in the natural realm. Begin to declare your personal truths today. Don't let another minute go by where you believe the lie. The devil is a liar. My prayer is that guilt will no longer take your heart, mind, and soul captive. Let it go today!

Your Personal Lies: _____

_____

_____

_____

_____

_____

_____

Your Personal Truths: _____

_____

_____

_____

_____

_____

Chapter 12

Tripped Up

Have you ever thought of something you would like to do—fulfill a dream or a desire before you leave this earth? Well, I have too. I have lived a very adventurous life. In 2012, I thought I would add something to my bucket list—a 5K. Yep, I wanted to accomplish this goal before I turned 50. It was crazy, especially when I never considered myself a runner. I was a cheerleader. I used to think 50 was old until I reached it. Now it was just a number. I never actually thought I would fulfill this dream, but I am that girl who once she puts her mind to it, you can consider it done.

One day while riding in the car, I just randomly spoke out loud to Rick that I wanted to run a 5K. He chuckled and said, "No way."

I said, "Yes, I have been thinking about this for some time, and now I am going to start training for it, so I can run my first 5K before I turn 50." I was giving myself about 10 months to train. I downloaded the app on my phone: "Couch to 5K." I was committed.

One of my closest friends, Pam Tarver, was turning 50 a few months later. She posted on Facebook all her running accomplishments with her fun 5Ks. I thought, *well, if she can do it, so can I.* I was envious of her accomplishments and determination. She could run for miles at a time. I wanted to as well.

Now, if you haven't run before, let me prepare you—it's very tough. It takes time to build up to reach your goal of three miles. I bought new running shoes, a cute outfit (of course), and put my headphones in and started trotting . . . yes, that is exactly what it was, a trot. I was completely out of breath, my side would hurt, and I was exhausted and out of shape. But I was determined to reach my goal.

I would call Pam, completely out of breath for her to coach me on completing what I had started.

The person talking on the app will tell you to jog; I trotted for a few minutes to build up to the full three miles, or 5K. Every day I would walk, trot, or run the greenway in our city and follow my app coach. Some days were easier than others. I found out that Lee University was having a 5K for their Homecoming in November 2012. I signed up. My stubbornness came in handy for this adventure. I trained for months and built my endurance to reach my goal of running in my first 5K.

It was an early, cold November morning. I was excited, but anxious. I had never even signed up for one, much less know what to do. Thoughts ran through my head about looking stupid. But I had a new outfit and looked the part, so all was right with the world. Rick supported me, but wasn't too happy about having to get up so early, too. "Don't they have afternoon 5Ks?" He is a funny guy. All the other runners had buddies. Well, I didn't. I was trying to look like I knew what I was doing. I looked around and people were stretching, so of course, I did too.

Watching from a distance, much to my surprise, I got this tap on my back. It was my best friend and personal running coach, Pam Tarver. She was my motivation. She got up early that morning to surprise me. I squealed, yep, I screamed like a girl jumping up and down like it was Christmas morning. I was so elated to know I wasn't running alone. For 35 plus years, Pam and I have journeyed life together. Sometimes, the roads were scary, unfair, troubling, and rough, but we always knew we had each other's back—regardless. We always had a blast no matter what we did. Laughter was always our common denominator. I always tried to make her laugh, and she would do the same for me. I did it! I ran, trotted, my first 5K before I turned 50, but it didn't come without opposition. But, I'm used to opposition. I can now check this adventure off my bucket list.

I was 30 when King was born. My body wasn't very healthy from my younger days and the way I had treated it when I had the eating disorder. My eating habits weren't healthy either. We lived in a three-story home, so when I brought King home from the hospital, I had to climb stairs. Having a cesarean didn't help. My body was very weak and not healing very quickly. It took my body about a year to even get normal, whatever normal means, after his birth. With the lack of sleep, not eating right, recovering from surgery, I was out of shape and physically exhausted. Rick was trying to hold down the fort with the staffing company while I took care of King pretty much by myself until he would come home from work. I am always protective of Rick's stress level, so I didn't want to add to it.

My core stomach muscles weren't very strong and I was trying to rebuild them. One day while I was downstairs in Brandon's room, I picked up the lid of a rubbing alcohol bottle. Much to my surprise, I realized with a loud moan, I couldn't raise myself back up. My back was hurting so badly; it was worse than the pain of childbirth. I had to crawl to the phone and call Rick to please pray. I told him, "Something isn't right." He took me to a chiropractor that took X-rays of my back. The X-rays showed I had two bulging discs. I was walking crooked from trying to compensate from the pain of standing straight. The doctor required me to come back two times a day to try to straighten my back. But I wasn't prepared for the next six weeks.

One morning after trying to get out of bed, the pain was so bad and my back was so out of alignment, lifting anything great or small was not an option. I had to crawl wherever I went, which for me now was only to the bathroom or to the car to go to the chiropractor and back home. King was way too heavy for me now, and he was only about 10 lbs. I moved to our bedroom what I needed in order to take care of him, and we managed to work from the floor. Going to the restroom to bend over was almost more than I could bear. It is amazing how much we use our stomach muscles and how hard it is to manage when our core is out of shape.

There are many spiritual parallels to our natural body, when our natural bodies are out of sync with our spirit. We must focus on the balance of life with mind, soul, body, and spirit. So many people focus on just one of the aspects. If we truly want to be a balanced person, embracing all the aspects will help in the proper function of our lives. I have heard a lot of preachers preach on just the spirit, but if we focus on just the spirit and not all three, we then become unbalanced. I truly believe moderation in all things. How can you fulfill your purpose if your body isn't healthy? What good is your calling if you have no energy to fulfill it, or you're so sick you can't even get out of bed?

What I learned from training for the 5K was my body was getting older and I had to do certain things to make sure I could fulfill my commitment. I learned quickly, I needed to drink more water when running, so my body wouldn't cramp up. Our bodies are made up of 75 percent water, so if we don't replenish it with the water we lose when we sweat, we will be dehydrated and cramp. I could always tell when I was dehydrated, because my side would hurt so badly I would have to stop, rest, drink more water, and walk the cramp out. The other thing I learned about my body was my knees and back could not endure the pounding like they could when I was younger. I would have to ice my knees from the swelling if I ran and walked more than 4 miles. My mother-in-love once told me, "Getting older isn't for sissies." And I completely agree.

I continued to run, or trot after the 5K. Running made me feel free for some reason. I could get into my own world and rhythm. I was on the greenway one morning when I noticed my shoe was untied. When I looked down, immediately I heard that still small voice say: "The Enemy of your soul wants to trip you up. He wants you to look down instead of looking up. That is where your strength comes from. He tries to trip you with life's issues to cause you to stumble, but stay the course and keep your eyes on Me. Don't get tripped up by his tactics. He is a deceiver."

I cherish these teachable moments. I want to always be a student, learning to be a better person—the person Jesus wants me to be. He is my mentor, teacher, best friend, intercessor, Savior, and so much more. When I hear that still small voice in my inner man, I am so encouraged to know that I don't ever have to face a challenging situation without my sweet personal Holy Ghost coaching, encouraging, and comforting me with His words of hope, strength, and love. I've learned that when I hear His whisper, He is close. If He yells, then it means He is far away. I need to always hear His whisper.

I raised my children to keep their ears open because sweet Holy Ghost has something He wants to teach us in every situation. King was 3 years old, and I was teaching him the art of listening to the Holy Ghost. He was in our oversized bathtub just chilling one evening.

I asked him, "King, what is Holy Ghost saying to you today?"

He thought for a moment and his response was priceless. He said, "Oh, Momma, He is telling me how much He loves me."

My response was, "Yes, King, He loves you very much. What else is he saying?"

He pondered for a moment, like only he can do, and said "Momma, He is telling me to tell you to go get me a Popsicle." I laughed so hard, but of course, I went and got him a Popsicle. Probably a little manipulation went along with that response. The apple doesn't fall far from the tree.

As a student of my faith, what I have come to understand is my faith can't be dictated by my circumstances, or I will be unstable.

My best friend Pam Tarver, whom I introduced to you earlier in this chapter, sent this to me. She didn't even know she was mentioned in this book, much less know the name of the chapter she was in. I love it when Father confirms His Word. God said, "What you tripped over last year you will leap over this year. If sickness, debt, or discord tripped you up, this year get ready to leap."

Ironically in my quiet time, I was instructed to read the story in Luke 1 (NLT) of the birth announcement of John the Baptist and Jesus. This is how it reads.

Luke 1

The Birth of John the Baptist Foretold

When Herod was king of Judea, there was a Jewish priest named Zechariah. He was a member of the priestly order of Abijah, and his wife, Elizabeth, was also from the priestly line of Aaron. Zechariah and Elizabeth were righteous in God's eyes, careful to obey all of the Lord's commandments and regulations. They had no children because Elizabeth was unable to conceive, and they were both very old.

One day Zechariah was serving God in the Temple, for his order was on duty that week. As was the custom of the priests, he was chosen by lot to enter the sanctuary of the Lord and burn incense. While the incense was being burned, a great crowd stood outside, praying.

While Zechariah was in the sanctuary, an angel of the Lord appeared to him, standing to the right of the incense altar. Zechariah was shaken and overwhelmed with fear when he saw him. But the angel said, "Don't be afraid, Zechariah! God has heard your prayer. Your wife, Elizabeth, will give you a son, and you are to name him John. You will have great joy and gladness, and many will rejoice at his birth, for he will be great in the eyes of the Lord. He must never touch wine or other alcoholic drinks. He will be filled with the Holy Spirit, even before his birth. And he will turn many Israelites to the Lord their God. He will be a man with the spirit and power of Elijah. He will prepare the people for the coming of the Lord. He will turn the hearts of the fathers to their children, and he will cause those who are rebellious to accept the wisdom of the godly."

Zechariah said to the angel, "How can I be sure this will happen? I'm an old man now, and my wife is also well along in years."

Then the angel said, "I am Gabriel! I stand in the very presence of God. It was he who sent me to bring you this good news! But now, since you didn't believe what I said, you will be silent and unable to speak until the child is born. For my words will certainly be fulfilled at the proper time."

Meanwhile, the people were waiting for Zechariah to come out of the sanctuary, wondering why he was taking so long. When he finally did come out, he couldn't speak to them. Then they realized from his gestures and his silence that he must have seen a vision in the sanctuary.
When Zechariah's week of service in the Temple was over, he returned home. Soon afterward his wife, Elizabeth, became pregnant and went into seclusion for five months. "How kind the Lord is!" she exclaimed. "He has taken away my disgrace of having no children."

The Birth of Jesus Foretold

In the sixth month of Elizabeth's pregnancy, God sent the angel Gabriel to Nazareth, a village in Galilee, to a virgin named Mary. She was engaged to be married to a man named Joseph, a descendant of King David. Gabriel appeared to her and said, "Greetings, favored woman! The Lord is with you!"

Confused and disturbed, Mary tried to think what the angel could mean. "Don't be afraid, Mary," the angel told her, "for you have found favor with God! You will conceive and give birth to a son, and you will name him Jesus. He will be very great and will be called the Son of the Most High. The Lord God will give him the throne of his ancestor David. And he will reign over Israel forever; his Kingdom will never end!"

Mary asked the angel, "But how can this happen? I am a virgin."

The angel replied, "The Holy Spirit will come upon you, and the power of the Most High will overshadow you. So the baby to be born will be holy, and he will be called the Son of God. What's more, your relative Elizabeth has become pregnant in her old age! People used to say she was barren, but she has conceived a son and is now in her sixth month. For the word of God will never fail."

Mary responded, "I am the Lord's servant. May everything you have said about me come true." And then the angel left her.

Mary Visits Elizabeth

A few days later Mary hurried to the hill country of Judea, to the town where Zechariah lived. She entered the house and greeted Elizabeth. At the sound of Mary's greeting, Elizabeth's child leaped within her, and Elizabeth was filled with the Holy Spirit.

Elizabeth gave a glad cry and exclaimed to Mary, "God has blessed you above all women, and your child is blessed. Why am I so honored, that the mother of my Lord should visit me? When I heard your greeting, the baby in my womb jumped for joy. You are blessed because you believed that the Lord would do what he said."

The Magnificat: Mary's Song of Praise

Mary responded,

"Oh, how my soul praises the Lord.
    How my spirit rejoices in God my Savior!
For he took notice of his lowly servant girl,
    and from now on all generations will call me blessed.
For the Mighty One is holy,
    and he has done great things for me.
He shows mercy from generation to generation
    to all who fear him.
His mighty arm has done tremendous things!
    He has scattered the proud and haughty ones.
He has brought down princes from their thrones
    and exalted the humble.
He has filled the hungry with good things
    and sent the rich away with empty hands.
He has helped his servant Israel
    and remembered to be merciful.
For he made this promise to our ancestors,
    to Abraham and his children forever."

Mary stayed with Elizabeth about three months and then went back to her own home.

The Birth of John the Baptist

When it was time for Elizabeth's baby to be born, she gave birth to a son. And when her neighbors and relatives heard that the Lord had been very merciful to her, everyone rejoiced with her.

When the baby was eight days old, they all came for the circumcision ceremony. They wanted to name him Zechariah, after his father. But Elizabeth said, "No! His name is John!"

"What?" they exclaimed. "There is no one in all your family by that name." So they used gestures to ask the baby's father what he wanted to name him. He motioned for a writing tablet, and to everyone's surprise he wrote, "His name is John." Instantly Zechariah could speak again, and he began praising God.

Awe fell upon the whole neighborhood, and the news of what had happened spread throughout the Judean hills. Everyone who heard about it reflected on these events and asked, "What will this child turn out to be?" For the hand of the Lord was surely upon him in a special way.

Zechariah's Prophecy

Then his father, Zechariah, was filled with the Holy Spirit and gave this prophecy:
"Praise the Lord, the God of Israel,
      because he has visited and redeemed his people.
He has sent us a mighty Savior
      from the royal line of his servant David,
just as he promised
      through his holy prophets long ago.
Now we will be saved from our enemies
      and from all who hate us.
He has been merciful to our ancestors
      by remembering his sacred covenant—
the covenant he swore with an oath
      to our ancestor Abraham.
We have been rescued from our enemies
      so we can serve God without fear,
in holiness and righteousness
      for as long as we live.
"And you, my little son,
      will be called the prophet of the Most High,
      because you will prepare the way for the Lord.
You will tell his people how to find salvation
      through forgiveness of their sins.
Because of God's tender mercy,
      the morning light from heaven is about to break upon us,
to give light to those who sit in darkness and in the shadow of death,
      and to guide us to the path of peace."

John grew up and became strong in spirit. And he lived in the wilderness until he began his public ministry to Israel.

What if God, your heavenly Father, is asking you to leap? I learn better when I use acronyms, so I have created one for you, hopefully it will help you remember. The word is LEAP.

The letter **L** is for **listen**. Listen to what your heavenly Father is asking you to leap toward. He has birthed greatness inside of you to be an overcomer; to reach your highest potential; to conquer your dreams; to be creative again; to share your story with a stranger; to begin to believe again, regardless of your age; and to live in faith, not fear. The Bible says, "My sheep know My voice" (John 10:27). I challenge you to listen, today, right now, to what Father is speaking to you.

The letter **E** is for **explore**. Explore the words of Jesus through the Bible and ask Him to confirm His will and words over you and what you are to leap toward. Whatever He leads you toward, He will not abandon you to figure it out on your own. He will reveal the secret, the hidden things to you so you will know which way to go.

The letter **A** is for **adventurous**. Life is full of adventures. To some, life is full of obstacles. It just depends on how you look at your circumstances and daily challenges. To me, I always see the glass half full, never half empty. God knew Mary and Elizabeth were adventurous women because He knew He could trust them with what He was developing and birthing in their wombs. He knew they would look at their circumstances as adventures instead of obstacles. Along with every blessing comes a burden. If you will endure the burden, you will receive the blessing. They could have made the choice for God to pick someone else to birth these world changers, but they decided they would accept the call. No matter what came against them, they were going to fulfill the words spoken over them. John the Baptist leaped just being in the presence of Jesus while he was still in the womb.

The letter **P** is for **promise**. God's promises to us, His children, are yes and amen. He will fulfill what He has promised over you if you will dare to believe again. Perhaps you've been told by your doctors that you won't be able to bear a child—your promise. Or, perhaps one business failed, so you feel crippled and paralyzed and can't leap because of fear and failure. I am asking you today, to be courageous, take the leap of faith and trust; Father has made a provision for the promises to be fulfilled in your life. I can promise you, He will not fail you.

106

Tripped Up

My prayer for you is just like John the Baptist leaped in Elizabeth's womb when Jesus was inside the womb of Mary, somehow what you are birthing in your womb will leap from the writings of these pages. I pray you are inspired to leap with me, and not get tripped up by the lies of your past.

My faith is built on the foundation of the words of my Savior. He wrote us a book of instructions on how to live with His blessings, but it's our responsibility to read and obey it. What is Father trying to say to you? Will you take the time to listen and obey? Don't be tripped up by the lies of your Enemy. Know your truths. They will set you free. Psalm 32:8 says, "I will instruct you and teach you in the way you should go; I will counsel you with my loving eye on you" (NIV). Follow His lead and you will never get tripped up.

Self-Awareness: I want to encourage you to step outside your comfort zone and do something you desire that perhaps you've never done before. Maybe it's writing a blog or a book, knitting, or building something with your own hands. Whatever it may be, let me encourage you to just do it. Take time out to search your heart and see what you may want to accomplish in this life and do it for you. You deserve it. You can do all things through Christ who gives you strength. What have you told yourself you cannot do? Just believe you can; see it, do it, and achieve it!

Personal Lies: _____

_____

_____

_____

_____

_____

_____

Personal Truths: _____

_____

_____

_____

_____

_____

_____

_____

Chapter 13

Inspired

When God gave me my two oldest children, Ryan and Lacey, at 26 years old, I never realized what life would look like as a mother to them. I had always considered them my gift from above, and I grew more in love with them as the years went by. I so desperately wanted them to be my blood. I wanted to be their healer and take all their pain away, instantly. I wanted so badly to be the Mom to them that when life caused them pain, a Mother's love would take it away or help relieve it, at least. But once again, God had a different plan. His plan was to allow life's challenges to develop them into amazingly strong adults. My honor and personal responsibility was, and is, to pray for them daily and love them through the good times and bad.

I am so inspired by all my children. To watch them grow up, pursue God's will for their individual lives and profess Jesus as their own, is a parent's greatest gift. I hated to watch them go through tragic times in their teens, but ultimately I knew I had a confident assurance that whatever journey they would choose, they would eventually find their way back home to the heart of God.

My husband, Rick, is a very strong, intelligent, God-fearing man. I have watched him walk through life with such integrity. Even when people did him wrong, he still did the right thing. Prayer and unconditional love is what has kept this family together. Rick and I decided early in our marriage, we would focus on our family being successful rather than putting all our effort into building an empire with our business. Our children would be our trophies, and truly they are.

I loved to get up early before anyone else and pray. I had my own prayer room dedicated to just Jesus and me; actually, it was my war room. I remember one morning specifically praying for Ryan. I have such great respect for him. His personal story of how he has developed a relationship with Jesus Christ is so fascinating. But now, we were praying him through a rough place in his life. He was carrying the burden of his life and childhood and all the disappointments with him and was living hate out loud. He was angry. And he had, in my opinion, all the reason to be. Life was unfair to him, and his sister, Lacey.

I remember one night we got a phone call, and he told us he had broken his foot or ankle. We thought maybe he had gotten into an accident or fallen off a motorcycle or something, but no, he was playing basketball and kicked the bleachers and broke something in his ankle. Anger was controlling him.

While I was praying to my heavenly Father, He began to show me something that I held onto through the rough times of Ryan's life. He showed me this beautiful man, standing in front of a large congregation. This person had on a casual suit looking very handsome. I asked Father, "Who is this man?"

Father's response was, "That's Ryan." I was amazed at what God was going to do in his life, yet didn't know the day or hour this transformation would happen.

Ryan had moved back to Cleveland and was attending Lee University at this time in his life. He was living off campus, doing his own thing, but would come home when he got hungry and needed a hot meal from his daddy. Rick is an incredible cook. In fact, all my children ask me not to cook. Most of the time I burn everything and the smoke alarm will go off.

During his college life at Lee, he was tapped to be a part of a fraternity. While enduring the weekend of induction, Ryan decided to write 666 on his forehead. His rebellious heart was ruling his life. It was during induction that God became real to Ryan, and he accepted Jesus as his personal Savior.

When my heavenly Father showed me in a vision this beautiful man, wearing a casual suit, standing and proclaiming the good news of Jesus Christ, I was elated with joy. I didn't even know this was part of his story at the time. God is faithful. Prayer works. Ryan found his beautiful bride, Andrea Simmons, at Lee University who loves him and Jesus. What was so cool is, Andrea loved him from a distance and prayed for him for two years before they married in 1999. They have given us three adorable grandchildren, Jeremiah, Jordan Faith, and Journey Grace, whom we love beyond words. They both are incredible parents. They are working in a church together serving God, helping others find Jesus. Ryan is a pastor, and Andrea leads worship. She sings like an angel, and will forever be my angel. She loves my son, my gift from above.

Lacey was our only girl. She and Ryan were very close. They were all each other knew at times. Yes, Rick was around, but he was struggling with his own challenges, much less having to raise two young children alone, not to mention a teenager. They clung to each other whenever they were together, because at times, they were separated to go live with other family members. Rick's previous marriage was troubled, and so were the children. God hates divorce, but loves divorced people. To some, that may seem hard to understand, but it is true. It is never God's delight for two people to end a marriage covenant, but when they do, God doesn't divorce them. He continues to love them, but hates the sorrow they are going to bring upon their lives. Divorce hurts everyone involved.

Lacey was hurting inside and as close as she would allow me to get, I would ease my way in, without her feeling I was intruding. She never knew what a good relationship with a Mom looked like, and I sure wasn't trying to take her mom's place. I just wanted to be her friend when she needed one. Through the years, I have watched her endure unbelievable situations. She is a survivor. It's not my story to tell, so if Ryan and Lacey choose to tell their stories and write a book, I will cheer them on. But with her permission, I will tell this part of her story.

At this season in her life, she was dating a guy that didn't believe like we did in Jesus. In fact, he was an atheist. How our baby girl found herself with an atheist, we don't know, but it broke our hearts. He was a history major and lacked the belief that Jesus was true.

Lacey was searching out her own salvation, but found a detour in her early years of college. She was attending a local state college, working on the river as a guide. That is how she found herself in a relationship with this guy. She brought him home, but we weren't giving our blessing in this relationship. Rick was furious; I do mean furious. We had walked her through many relationships with other guys. One of the guys she dated was planning to go into the ministry; however, he crushed her spirit and shattered her heart. In turn, this sent her down a spiraling decline of believing in a God-fearing relationship.

It took a very long time for her to recover from that relationship, and now she found herself with an atheist—what an extreme! Once again, we were interceding on her behalf to break the chains that kept her bound to this guy. Lacey graduated from the community college and moved out of town with him. We thought for sure his intent was to keep her away from her God-fearing parents, and we feared we had lost her forever. What is so cool about God is there is no distance with Him. He owns the universe. It didn't matter if she lived three hours away or three days away. Prayer has no border or boundaries. It can penetrate to the heart from any distance. She lived with him for three years. Guess what we did? We prayed for three years without ceasing.

God began to open her eyes. The last thing we ever wanted was for her to live with a heart of rejection. Rejection had already taken root in her heart from her mother. As parents, all we wanted to do was protect her from man rejecting her too. As we know, the One who loved her the most and would never reject her was Jesus, but she would have no part of Him. She was so intellectually smart. Science and math were her greatest subjects in school, along with her being captain on the debate team. While in this devastating relationship, we could sense she was debating the truths she was taught while growing up about the love of Jesus.

Eventually, she moved from East Tennessee after graduating to live in Florida. She broke up with the atheist. It was prayer that changed her stony heart to be soft and pliable. You could see her quest was for something greater. She had personally seen God perform miracles in our blended family.

She found her way back home to the heart of Jesus. Her walk with Jesus inspired me more than I could ever begin to explain. One day she was talking with Jesus, and said, "If you will grant me the ability to play instruments, I will give you all the glory." Sure enough, a little girl with no rhythm now plays the drums, guitar, and piano. I am truly amazed and inspired by her tenacity to hold on, even when she was dropped, like Mephibosheth, by the one who should have been protecting her.

Lacey married, and once again faced rejection from her husband. He found someone else to love besides her. During this troublesome time, she never lost her faith. She called us to pray for a divine intervention in their marriage. She tried, but he left. She is single, now. Watching her completely surrender her life and be an incredible mother to our two beautiful grandbaby girls, Hailey and Hannah, is priceless. She went on to get her master's degree and worked in the educational system in West Palm Beach, Florida. What looked like tragedy turned into triumph, because she decided not to give up but to give in to her Creator. She knew God had a plan, and His plan for her life is to give her a hope and a future. (See Jeremiah 29:11.)

Both Ryan and Lacey have hearts of gold. They are sensitive to the heart of Jesus and long to please their Savior. I am continually reminded about where they got their beautiful hearts. On Rick's sixty-second birthday, we were working at the office at iKruit Staffing. He walked into my office with tears streaming down his cheek. "Babe," he said, "will you please write a check out for $100 for this man I just interviewed?"

"Of course," I said.

He proceeded to tell me the man's story. It was like some of the giants Rick faced earlier in his life.

When Rick turned 30, he felt very depressed, hopeless, and wanted an end to his misery. He decided to drink a fifth of whisky to try to drink his sorrows away. The Enemy of his soul was constantly trying to convince him that he was a failure and to somehow end his life. On another occasion, he was tormented with thoughts of taking his own life by throwing himself before a semi to stop the pain he was feeling inside. Like me, he was a preacher's kid who didn't know how to live with the Jesus his father preached about every Sunday. Thank God, He had a plan for Rick's life.

Just one decision made differently would have eliminated the possibility of our ever being a happy blended family today. If Rick would have succumbed to the torment inside and obeyed that voice of the Enemy trying to steal his life, it would have robbed Ryan and Lacey of having their father. It would have likewise robbed me from being his wife and their mother, Brandon from being his son, and King from ever being born. And finally, it would have robbed the impact our children have on today's society. Humbly I say, with God's help, we have raised World Changers.

Back to the gentleman in our office: What brought Rick to tears was the similarity of their stories. The man proceeded to tell him that the day he was going to put a bullet in his head, we called him for an interview, giving him hope. He came in the next day for an interview, and that's when he began to tell Rick his sorrows. Filled with compassion, and understanding this man's private pain, Rick proceeded to encourage the man with hope in Jesus. When Rick handed him the check, the man's response was, "No one has ever done this for me before." Rick was Jesus with skin on to that man that day. He shared with him hope in Jesus, and Jesus would help see him through, just like Jesus did for him. What a beautiful birthday present to be able to introduce Jesus to someone else. Ministry isn't just from the pulpit; it is in the marketplace as well. The people who come through our doors for employment may never enter the threshold of the doors of a church. We want to be "Jesus with skin on" to them.

For me, being married to Rick is a dream come true. I knew love growing up, but when I chose to embrace the approval of man rather than the approval of God, detours began in my life. I wanted man's applause over God's. In return, I was empty, lost, bound, and afraid. What I have learned through the years is when Rick and I got married, we made a covenant rather than a contract in marriage. So, you ask, what is the difference? The difference is when you make a covenant, you gain life, love, and eternity. I made a covenant to Rick, Ryan, Lacey, and to God the day we joined hands in the circle at our wedding. My covenant was that I would love them with all my heart. Our marriage is more than a contract that can be broken by a judge in the courts of man; it is a covenant, a vow for life.

All our children have taught me something. I learn from them every day. For example, Ryan has taught me what unconditional love looks like. He loved me even though I wasn't his birth mother, Lacey too. Lacey also has taught me what true surrender and perseverance look like through the eyes of Jesus. She has survived all the obstacles she has faced in life, with Jesus right beside her. Rejection no longer defines her. One of her passions is playing all her instruments in worship. I love to see her rejoicing in her Savior's love and acceptance. She's my only girl, and I can't thank God enough for her in my life. We are best friends now. Brandon has taught me what the face of grace looks like. I saved his life, and he saved mine. I didn't always do what was right, but God saw I needed grace and gave Brandon to me. When King was born, he taught me what it meant to be courageous and purposeful. He taught me to be organized and plan, even though he wasn't planned and was our biggest surprise; he is our sweet baby boy.

When King was just a baby, I must be honest, I wasn't sure if he was going to like me. His temperament was just like his daddy's: melancholy, not liking change and spur of the moment transitions. Me? I love change. I could change furniture, cars, and material things every three to four years. King was my planner; he was organized and structured. I wasn't. I had to learn those traits. Rick played a huge part in my learning them and so did my purposeful child. You couldn't just snatch King up and say, "Come on we're going somewhere." You had to prepare him for everything, and make sure he was OK with it, or he would get very upset. One example, he was so picky, I had to try five nipples after breastfeeding until finally he liked one. What a glorious day! Just wait until he has children: paybacks! (Just kidding.) I will be there to coach him through it. I know he will need it. I was struggling thinking about what I was going to do with this toddler whom I was not sure even liked me, much less how to deal with his personality. Until one glorious day, I went to get my hair done.

I was exhausted, tired, worn down physically, mentally, and emotionally. Relaxing in my beautician's chair, I told my hair stylist what was going on with my terrific two-year-old and me. She said three words that changed my life. She said, "Sandi, you need to GET A TIMER."

A timer?

She said, "Yes, children that need structure get frustrated when you do something spontaneously. They need to prepare their brain for the next upcoming event, even if it is something small."

So, I did just that. Immediately after leaving my hair salon, I went to the store and purchased a cheap white timer. I still have it to this day. This started a new way of life for me. And much to my surprise, it was a miracle worker. I set that timer for him to take a bath, put his shoes on, and take off his Texas Ranger Chuck Norris cowboy outfit and boots to go to bed. Believe it or not, it worked every time. I was amazed. I thought I had died and gone to heaven. The struggling was over.

If you have a child with the melancholy temperament that needs to think things through and process his next step, I encourage you with these four words that I lived by, "This too shall pass" and "Go buy a timer." King is an amazing man. I honestly have never met anyone like him before. When he sets his mind to do something, he will do it. He is such a great son; Rick and I can't believe he is ours, especially knowing our history. Rick teases and says we need to get his blood checked to see if he is ours. But trust me; I have the scar to prove he is mine. Oh, the faithfulness of God! I would have never dreamed my life would be this wonderful, but it isn't a dream; it's my reality. God has restored my youth, my truth. No more shame.

Brandon has married a wonderful, beautiful girl named, Reagan Smith. On December 12, 2012, we celebrated the birth of his first child, Truly Noa Perritte in Tacoma, Washington. On October 14, 2015, we added number seven to our grands list—a beautiful baby boy named Shepherd Rory-Smith Perritte. The Roy part of his name comes from my daddy. I love that. His legacy lives on. They both serve in a church faithfully as pastors, sharing the love and good news of Jesus Christ.

Reagan is a loving, kind, selfless, wife, mother, daughter-in-love, and friend. She loves her faith, and family. Thank you, Reagan, for saying yes in marrying Brandon and being a great unifier in this blended family. Cache will always be one of my favorite stores because of you.

Our family circle has grown. King married a beautiful girl named BriAnna. She is so genuine. They moved to Texas to work at pursuing ministry as youth pastors. We knew early on, if anyone could handle King, Bri could.

After they were dating a few months, Bri and I were developing a strong bond. We loved her, and besides, she was a cheerleader, too. Of course, we bonded. She was battling her own fears and would occasionally ask my advice. I asked her if she would write her story and she agreed. Here is Bri's very own personal truth.

Invisible

I've never questioned the existence of God. I've always seen Him in everything around me: the first bite of a strawberry, blooming flowers, pregnant bellies. You name it; I could picture the Creator furrowing His brow while He gently molded it into existence.

Regardless of how lovely that ideology sounds, the issue was that I saw only what was happening around me. I was an outlier, smiling from a distance at the ways God was working in the lives around me. Or, how about this one? If I were in the movie Harry Potter, I wouldn't be Hermione or Luna, or even Padma Patil (was she even listed in the credits?), I would have been one of the students in Hufflepuff that had a millisecond of airtime during a Quidditch game.

Either actively or passively, we all are faced with two questions. The first: "Is there an existence of an all-powerful God, who separated light from darkness, spoke everything into being, and not only created me, but knew me before I was in my mother's womb?" (I got a gold star on that one). The second, and most mystifying: "Could this awesome Being love me?" This is the question that had me stumped, and this is how the Enemy isolated me for almost ten years.

I don't remember the first time that Satan whispered in my ear, but it probably sounded something like this: "You are all alone."

To which innocent, pig-tailed me would have replied: "No, I'm not, I have mommy and daddy, and Becky, and Mandy and Jackie..."

"No, you'll always be alone and you'll never belong."

Maybe the first time I didn't believe it, but eventually I gave up the rebuttal and didn't have anything left to stand on.

I don't blame 10-year-old me, how was I (unbeknownst to his taking thoughts captive) to face the master of all lies? I picture myself in a courtroom, glasses, and Limited Too, unsure of why I'm there. Just as I'm about to state my case, a slick Harvard alum with a Ph.D. cuts me off and persuades the jury in his favor. I must pay the price for a crime never committed, and the price is isolation. The Enemy doesn't have to whisper in my ear anymore, the lies have become my mantra.

Fast-forward six years, and that innocent ten-year-old isn't so innocent anymore. Still believing the lies of the Enemy, and at the same time, believing in God, I roamed the halls of public high school, which was a battleground in itself. I feared walking into a class full of people and finding a seat next to someone, and, more than anything, when the teacher would tell us to "partner up." When I was invited to parties, I would feel as though everyone were watching my every move, and I would leave early without saying goodbye, craving the alone time in my car. There, I would replay every word I said and how people would view me.

This continued in college. I not only feared, but avoided social situations. Regrettably, I spent a great deal of time in my dorm by myself; while my roommates did social things I deemed "too awkward" for me.

When I think back on those memories, I realize that I viewed myself in third-person. I did everything in the image that I perceived others to have of me. I made excuses by saying, "people just don't get me" or "we just have different personalities." Surprisingly, I had no idea any of this was an issue, and Satan sat back and smiled as I isolated myself further and became bitter toward the people God created and loves.

I think you get the picture. I was a total mess. A Christian failure, if you will. So, it only makes sense that I met my husband at this time.

Enter King Kramer: social butterfly, lover of all things people, and future pastor. Let me just pause and comment on how ironic it is that God would take someone so opposed to relationships with people and pair her with someone who lived for it. Picturing me as a pastor's wife was just a ludicrous notion. Not only that, but it's a popular belief that you will not meet your spouse until you get it together. I most certainly did not have it all together, but God blessed me with someone who helped me see that the way I felt when I walked into a room was not the way God intended it.

At the beginning of our relationship, I tried very hard to keep up with forming new relationships with all the people in his life, attending Wednesday night church services, and going to small groups. He had no idea that I dreaded going all week because I was so afraid of people and what they thought of me or that I couldn't wait to dart out of my seat and into the comfort of my car when it was all over.

At first I was relieved that it wasn't normal to feel this way. I was glad that it had a name—anxiety. Then, I felt angry that I had to go through the steps to change. I would rather stay the same than face my fears. Isn't it strange that we can prefer to live in darkness when God wants much more for us?

The worst part of anxiety is that to get through it, you just must do that which you fear. To not be afraid of people, I had to go where people were, which in my case was church. Not only that, but I had to interact with those people and even try to love them.

If you have experienced anxiety, you know that you can't just "buck up." You don't just decide to have a better attitude about the situation and move on. You need complete restoration. I'm so thankful we have a direct line to the One who offers all the restoration we need.

Not knowing what was ahead, I put on my eye black and got ready to make war on the lies of the Enemy. I made booklets and filled them with the truths of Scripture. I memorized and meditated on these truths and pulled them out when I felt like running from the situation. What is most important, I allowed God to shape me into the person He had called me to be. He intended for me to be in relationship with others, not fighting battles by myself.

On October 31, 2012, while my mother-in-law, Sandi Kramer, was washing my feet and praying for me, the Lord freed me from the chains of social anxiety. I felt it inside my soul. I knew I would never have to walk through a room and fear what the people were thinking of me. I knew that everything had changed.

I also knew that I had to help others experience the freedom that I did. Not just with anxiety, but with any lie that the Enemy throws at them. The Lord loves us so much more than we can imagine and intends for us to be free. The only way we can truly experience freedom is to give Him our lives and allow Him to work through us.

I finally have my answer to my second question: "Does the Creator of the universe care for me?" A resounding, "yes"! He cares enough for me to take my mountain of an issue and squash it. He cares enough for me to redeem me from a pit of lies and a life of loneliness. He cares enough to erase the lies of ten years and replace them with loving truths. He cares.

What a beautiful story of our heavenly Father's love, grace, and truths He so desperately desires for us to walk in. I am so grateful the God of the universe saw that we needed BriAnna Catherine Anderson in this family. What a gift she is to us all. By the way, God has a sense of humor. She never wanted to ever be a pastor's wife. Guess what? She is a great one and has a beautiful servant's heart.

When King came home and said he found his love for life, he said, "Mom, I think I found someone who loves me more than you do." I said, laughingly, "Son that's impossible, but I want her to always keep trying."

When they got married, Rick and I were now entering the "empty- nest" phase of life, and I knew I had to cut the cord. Everyone was telling me to just let go. Well, that is much easier said than done, but I was trying not to be overbearing. One day I was conversing, praying with my heavenly Father, when in my spirit I heard Him say, *When you cut the cord and let go, Bri will tie it in a bow.* Right then, I knew all would be well with them. God had a huge plan, and I could just sit back and watch Him work out all things for their good.

Before they left for Texas, I went to a ministry meeting. A sweet lady was sharing a story. I wasn't sure why I was there until she gave the scriptures from Isaiah 42. Verse 1 starts out like this: "Take a good look at my servant; I'm backing him to the hilt. He's the one I chose, and I couldn't be more pleased with him." As you continue to read in verse 16 it says,

> But I'll take the hand of those who don't know the way, who can't see where they are going. I'll be a personal guide to them, directing them through unknown country.

I'll be right there to show them what roads to take, make sure they don't fall into the ditch. These are the things I'll be doing for them—sticking with them, not leaving them for a minute" (MSG).

I was overwhelmed by His confirming words to this mother's heart who loves her children more than life. I came home rejoicing and had to share my truths with Rick. He was amazed, listening as tears rolled down his face. Oh, how precious our heavenly Father is to give us such a confirmation that all is well. God truly cares.

Self-Awareness: What inspires you? Do you believe God has a plan for your life? Do you believe Jesus cares for you and about your future, where to go to college, who you will marry? Let me confidently assure you, He does. What lie have you believed for so long that hinders you from being inspired to take the next step in Jesus? Perhaps you are living to just get by, or you are going through the motions of life, but feel lifeless. Please know, Jesus has more for you. He is not done with you yet! Regardless of the lies you have believed, today is your new day! Write your personal lies, and then bury them in the truths of God's Word. Read Jeremiah 29:11, and put your name in this scripture. Say it out loud, every day. God has a plan for your life—hope, and a great future.

Personal Lies: _____

_____

_____

_____

_____

_____

_____

Personal Truths: _____

_____

_____

_____

_____

_____

_____

Chapter 14

Grace

Since my late 20s, I have felt the call of God on my life to pray. Sometimes, my heavenly Father would ask me to do things for a season. One time He asked me to get up an hour early while another time he asked me specifically to pray a scripture. My scripture over Rick for a very long time was, Isaiah 11:2: "The Spirit of the LORD will rest on him—the Spirit of **wisdom and of understanding**, the Spirit of counsel and of might, the Spirit of the **knowledge and fear of the LORD**" (NIV). While I was praying one morning I heard my sweet Father say, "You can do more on your knees that you can behind a platform right now." I knew I was called to a new season of prayer. I consider it an honor He would choose me to pray for His children. While I was enjoying my quiet time with Jesus in His presence, He said: "I want to talk to you about grace—My enduring grace for you."

I was raised more under law, but learning to abide and live in His grace was new to me. I knew I needed grace all my life, I just thought it was up to me to deserve it, and I knew I wasn't good enough to receive it. Today, I realize it's not up to me to be good enough; it's up to Jesus and He is more than good enough. He is MY grace. Jesus continued to share with me how important grace was, not just to receive, but to also give to others. He reminded me of a time in my life where His grace covered me.

I was single at the time, still searching, trying to understand how to live with Jesus when I found myself desperately in need of grace. I had decided to go out one night with a friend of mine. She and I went to a local restaurant where we had a bartender friend. I wasn't looking for trouble, most of the time. It just seemed to follow me or at least search me out. This night we sat at the bar. Our bartender friend was continually pouring us drinks. What I didn't know until later was he was putting our drink tab on the man's tab sitting at the end of the bar. He was already drunk and would never know how much his bill was. I know that is awful. Honestly, If I knew who this man was, I would pay him back, because I am sure when he got sober, he was shocked at the amount of his bill. We had been drinking quite a bit, but it didn't take much for me; I was a lightweight. For those of you who don't drink, a lightweight is someone who can't handle a lot of alcohol. I'm not sure how much I drank that night, I just knew I pushed my limit and we started heading home.

It was very late at night and my friend had already passed out in the car. We were on I-75, heading home from Chattanooga, Tennessee, when suddenly my tire blew. The car started spinning in the middle of the highway about three times, and then hit the side of the embankment smashing her side of the car. Immediately, I sobered up. I looked at my friend to check on her, and she was startled by the sound and tried to get herself together. For a minute or two, we just sat there in the dark wondering what we were going to do. I had already caused my parents so much pain there was no way I was going to get them involved in this mess. I got out of the car to assess the damages. It was awful. Her side of my car was smashed in so badly that my friend had to get out on my side. My tire was flat, and I didn't have any money to call someone to help tow my car. Fear gripped my heart because my daddy always told me, if I got caught drinking and driving, he would make me stay in jail for three days. I think he was using the three days to illustrate I needed a death, burial, and resurrection in my life. Thank goodness, there were no policemen around this late at night.

While I was out of the car thinking about what in the world I was going to do and who I could call for help, Jesus reminded me of a part of the story that brought me to tears. He said, "Remember when you got out of your car and you felt the wind of the semitruck pass you, brushing your hair in the wind."

I responded, "Yes, Sir."

He said, "It was my angels whom I have given charge over you to push your car out of the way of that semi and hit the embankment.

If your car would have stopped spinning in the middle of the road, you would have been hit, but my grace covered you and pushed you out of the way."

I'm sure my angels wanted to be reassigned to someone else after that night. I was always wearing them out.

Now in my life, it was just Brandon and me. I was single. Brandon would have been raised without his mom. Jesus' grace covered me, shielded me, and protected me. I am so very grateful Jesus oversees my destiny. It was this story that Jesus wanted me to see His hand was truly on my life. I wasn't alone; He was always with me. This was another side of the face of grace.

I was always that girl who felt she needed Jesus, but didn't know how to live with Him. I was too filthy. No one would ever love me because of my bad choices. I was the girl that when she got high, she asked the others at the party if they knew Jesus. I knew I needed Him, but didn't understand that the whole time while I was searching for Him, He was always in love with me.

A friend of mine that my daddy warned me about, asked me to be her babysitter. I was new in the city and thought to myself: *Sure, I need the money.* She didn't want to go to her boyfriend's house alone one night and asked me if I would go with her. She would find someone else to watch her son. I said, "Sure; sounds fun."

It was at UTC, University of Tennessee at Chattanooga. We were at the wrestling team's dorm rooms, which were more like apartments. She left me in a room with a bunch of wrestlers I didn't know. They were passing around what looked like a cigarette. Needless to say, it was laced with something—something that sent this little girl into hallucinations. Suddenly, the green carpet turned into grass. The grass then turned into bugs. The bugs started flying. I was petrified. I started going over to each wrestler asking them if they knew Jesus. I needed Him to get me out of here. I was never asked back, and I was completely fine with that.

As I get older, I can see the hand of God all through my life. Rick and I were struggling financially, and started a consulting company called, The Vision Group. We wanted to help train and mentor other business people on how they could go forward with their vision in business. One morning, I couldn't sleep. I was frustrated because it seemed like for every step we took forward; we took ten steps backwards. I was crying out to God, perhaps pouting, and in the sweet voice that I hear my Father speak, He said, "Sandi, I will take my hand off your life and allow you to do whatever you think is best for you. But if my hand is removed from you, you will crash and burn." Immediately, I cried out again for a whole different reason. I had tried living my life without Jesus in the past, and I wasn't successful. The sorrow that filled my heart was overwhelming.

I cried out, "No, Jesus, please, please keep Your hand on us. I can't do life without You. I don't want to do life without You." I am crazy about my Savior, now. I can't live a minute, a second without His breath and hand upon my life. He has been so faithful to me.

Sometimes we think we can orchestrate our lives better than God. When you say that out loud, you will understand how ridiculous it sounds. Do we understand whom we are talking about? The Creator of the universe who calls the stars into existence, parts the mountains from the waters, creates oceans and all the living things that reside in them, and we think we can do better with our lives?

My answer to that question is absolutely, "No way." God is sovereign. We may not always understand His ways or thoughts, because they are much more intelligent than ours. My challenge to you is to trust God with your life, circumstances, situations, children, and family—all that concerns you. He cannot and will not fail you, even if you don't understand His ways. We still have our consulting business. God has blessed us beyond measure. When I look back and see where He has brought this family, I can't stop crying from pure joy, gratitude, and amazement.

In 2005, I felt it was important to start mentoring girls. I wrote the book, *Identity Theft: Who's Behind the Mask*, for people to read my story about what I have been through, and hopefully encourage others. I was prophesied over when I was 16 that I would speak to the multitudes. I am still waiting for that prophecy to be fulfilled. Every day I try to inspire someone to be better today than they were yesterday. I look for my assignment. You never know when you entertain strangers, you may be encountering an angel.

iKruit Staffing demands most of my time. At this season of my life, I needed help in cleaning my house, so I found this amazing woman to help me. She was going through a rough time with her husband's health, children, and raising her grandchildren. It was a win for both of us. She needed the money; I needed her help. Over the years we grew in our relationship. She felt like family. She would clean my mother's house and my grandma's house. Her granddaughter needed a bit of coaching. She was struggling with the loss of her papa, who was the only real male figure in her life. Her heart was broken. She felt pieces of her heart would never mend again. She knew pain growing up, but none felt this painful. I understood her pain. Since I life-coach girls, I said "of course, let me see if we can help get her on the path to healing." With her permission, she has allowed me to let you read a few pages of her life.

Never Good Enough

If you look at many of the world's most successful people, you will find that they had some sort of rejection in their childhood. As a result, these people spend their entire lives working tirelessly to prove to themselves and to the world that they are worthy of love.

That is exactly how I was in college. I worked 35 hours a week, and spent hours upon hours studying so I could have perfect grades. When I did not get the coveted "A," I would feel such defeat. I remember one class in particular—physics, and it was excruciatingly difficult. I would spend anywhere from 10-12 hours studying for one test, not to mention the 3-5 hours I spent on the weekly homework assignments. I would go in to take my exams, and I would literally almost have a panic attack. When I looked over the test and realized that I didn't know any of the answers off the top of my head, and I often didn't even know the pathway to solve the problem, my breathing would increase, my eyes would fill up with tears, and my mind would fill up with terrifying words. "You're worthless. You are such a fraud. You are in this class with all these intelligent people, and you don't even deserve to be here. You are probably the dumbest person in this room, and let's not even talk about how you are psychotic. Why are you crying, you freak? You studied 12 hours and you still can't even do it, you piece of trailer trash." After these exams, I would get headaches because of how emotional I would become.

I think my obsession with academics came from the first time I ever made a B. I was in seventh grade, and I still remember getting in the car. My nana had just gotten off work. God love her. She was raising two kids on her retirement fund; she was stressed to the max. Her daughter was facing prison time, and here I came bopping along to the car. I had my report card in hand. My B was in math. (It's funny how that became my major in college and my profession now. Should we wonder if I am performance driven?) I told her the disappointment. Encouraging words were far from that car. I had let her down, and I could see it all over her face, and I could hear it in her silence. Fear of rejection and letting people down had driven me to work as hard as I possibly could, but with no consideration to my health, my sleep patterns, my emotional wellbeing, or my relationship with God.

But it wasn't just for my nana. I failed myself. Good isn't enough. Great isn't enough. I have to be the best. Nothing else will do, and, if I'm not the best, then I reject myself. The problem is I am frequently not the best.

What's interesting is I never felt my papa's rejection. He never was disgusted with me. I remember the night I told my grandparents about cutting. I showed them my arms. My nana and papa grew up in a different time period; cutting was associated with crazy people and demons. Yet, here was their little girl with cuts all up her arm. I remember pulling my sleeve up. The only thing my papa said was, "Why did you do that for?" He came to counseling with me. Oh, he was so good. My papa thought I hung the moon. He saw value in me. I will never forget his face when I would pull in the driveway. He would be sitting on the front porch, and his little eyes would light up. I loved that man. Papa always told me I was smart. He said he wished he could be smart like me. He said I was pretty. I know he had to, but I think he saw it. Needless to say, when we lost him to cancer, my world was shaken, as was my image of myself.

The thing about being performance-driven is that it doesn't work. I don't want to work, work, and work just to prove to myself that I'm not good enough. I need grace. I need mercy. I need the Lord to pull me in close, and I need to see my value in His eyes—just like I did in my papa's. I want to trust in what the Lord says about me, and then I want to walk on straight paths. I don't want to laboriously walk, *and never feel good enough, pretty enough, smart enough. Jesus is enough. I am learning to walk in that truth, daily.*

This beautiful, charismatic, loving, brilliant, good-enough young lady has now gone on to fulfilling her calling as a teacher, helping other students realize their value and self-worth. I just recently attended her wedding. She was a beautiful bride.

Self-Awareness: Have you ever thought about hurting, cutting, punishing yourself because of your inner thoughts, comparing yourself to other people? Or, listening to the liar of your soul tell you you're not valuable because someone left you, dropped you, and didn't protect you. Please write out three of your personal lies and follow up with three of your personal truths of what your heavenly Father says about you.

Personal Lies: _____

_____

_____

_____

_____

_____

_____

Personal Truths: _____

_____

_____

_____

_____

_____

_____

_____

Chapter 15

The Womb

Brandon was attending Lee University majoring in pastoral studies. It was during his counseling class, the revelation of the importance of the womb became so personal. I have always heard the baby feels in the womb what the mother feels, and also how important it is to bond in the womb by singing and playing music, which helps with the development of the baby. But when Brandon was asked to write a paper telling his story, his professor brought an "ah-ha" moment to him of why he struggled so much with rejection growing up.

His professor pulled him aside after class, fascinated by our story, and began to explain. What the professor and Brandon didn't know was the torment I experienced while carrying Brandon. After moving so far away from my family to North Dakota, the feelings of isolation and being alone were overwhelming. I was very young and still needed my family close to me. Here I was more than 3,000 miles away from home, young, pregnant, and both my hormones and my body were rapidly changing. Emotionally, I was a train wreck. What no one knew were the tormenting, demonically influenced dreams I had of walking into the kitchen, taking a large butcher knife, and stabbing my stomach repeatedly, killing us both. Struggling with the demonic spirit of death and the realization of having a child and all the responsibility that goes along with being a parent, I would wake up from the nightmare, gasp for breath, and thank God it was just that—a nightmare. I would get up, get dressed, and head out for work, keeping my secret to myself. If I shared what I saw or felt, I was afraid people would think I was crazy. The nightmares persisted for months, until the day he was born. My parents called after I delivered Brandon, and they told me they were on their way to see us from Tennessee. I told my daddy how much he weighed, and he said, "Good Lord, you had a toddler."

When Brandon's professor revealed the revelation of the womb to him, he shared this truth with me. Of course, I felt sorrowful that I had not bonded with him more during my pregnancy. I desperately wished that I could take back the pain and sorrow I had invoked on my son. As a mother, I never wanted my children to hurt. I would rather it had been me, than my babies. I had always thought Brandon felt rejection from being raised in a divorced home, and of course, that didn't help, but now, adding this dimension to his emotional state growing up made perfect sense. I began to pray against the root of rejection, asking my heavenly Father to surround him with the acceptance of His love and approval over him.

Recently, I got a text from King asking me when he began to experience fear. There was a war going on in his soul and he wanted to fight against it. I expressed to Rick the struggle King was facing. At first, we thought it was when he and his cousin Jessica at the age of 8 watched the movie, *Twister*. We had gone out to visit my sister's family, and they watched movies. I had no idea King watched this movie, much less how this movie impacted King's life for years. He had always been a very intuitive, sensitive, prophetic child. He would randomly speak a scripture verse, and sure enough it would line up with exactly what we were going through that day. Matthew 21:16 says, "Do you hear what these children are saying?" (NIV). We always tuned our ear to listen when King would speak something profound.

On one occasion, when King was about 7 or 8 we were walking in Walmart. King tugged at my leg and said, "Mommy, Jesus wants me to tell you to just trust Him." I said, "Oh, King, thank you, I do." Then, I proceeded to ask him, "Is He telling you to tell me something else? King replied, "No, Mommy, don't read into it, just trust Him."

However, after watching *Twister*, the spirit of fear developed within him to such a degree that for four years, we had to put a pallet by our bed for him. He was too afraid to sleep in his room, which led me to thinking about when King was a baby. We would rock him to sleep, place him gently in his bed, but every time, he would wake up crying—I mean crying for hours. Neither Rick nor I had ever known a child that would cry for so long. We would discipline him, thinking he was just a "strong-willed" child, and we were going to win this battle of the wills. Then, the revelation of the womb—Father so gently began to walk me through my pregnancy with King.

I wasn't a happy pregnant woman with King either. I realize I will have haters for writing this, but I can't deny my truths. I didn't have that kind of glow everyone else talks about. All I felt was how miserable I was from the baby being on my main artery to my brain, and passing out, or constantly being nauseated and throwing up. I also had to go to the hospital every week after our car wreck (45 minutes away), and this was getting annoying. So, as I begin to answer the question King had asked me about when he first began to feel fear, the spiritual revelation from all of this was—it was when King was in my womb. My fear was having a second-born child with the same genetic eye disorder as Brandon and being born blind. The Enemy of my soul would rehearse and taunt me over and over with the scripture from Job 3:25-26: "What I feared has come upon me; what I dreaded has happened to me. I have no peace, no quietness; I have no rest, but only turmoil" (NIV). So, you say, how is it that the devil could speak scripture to you and apply it to your life in a negative way?

When Jesus was in the wilderness, the Bible says in Matthew 4:1: "Then Jesus was led by the Sprit into the wilderness to be tempted by the devil" (NIV). The Spirit of the Lord led Jesus into the wilderness. The Spirit of the Lord was with Jesus; therefore, He was not alone. Just as the Spirit of the Lord is with us, if we have accepted Jesus as our Savior, then we are never alone. As you read more in the chapter, you will notice the devil speaks to Jesus by tempting him in the natural. Three times Jesus is approached by the devil in these passages—with bread, breath/life, and to bow down. In the first temptation, the devil was trying to tempt Jesus to break His fast and eat the bread to nourish the flesh with natural bread instead of sustaining bread of life from above. The second temptation was with breath/life. The devil was trying to get Jesus to take His own life by jumping off a cliff, saying His angels would save Him. Third, the devil tried to tempt Jesus to bow down and worship him as lord instead of His heavenly Father. The devil's main goal is to seduce and lure people to worship him instead of Jesus.

The Enemy of our soul, the devil, tries to come at us when we are most vulnerable—through our thoughts and mindset, trying to persuade us to renounce our personal beliefs. While carrying King, I embraced fear; therefore, he felt my emotional state. Now, he also fights fear. Immediately after I received this revelation, I called him to share with him this amazing truth. But I can't leave it there.

I started searching in the depth of my soul. For so long, I had always believed that my root of rejection developed when I was 16. Then suddenly, I remembered back in 2005 after I had shared my story at a women's conference, my mom made a personal confession that she had never spoken out loud before. The revelation of Brandon being rejected from the womb was convicting her to confess. Women were praying at the altar seeking the heart of God, and my sweet mom came over to me at the very end of the service. She said, "Sandi, I am so sorry." I was taken aback by the tears streaming down her face. She was barely able to speak because she was crying so hard. I asked, "What is it Momma?" I tried to console her, because her heart was so sorrowful; I had no idea what she was about to tell me. She proceeded to say, "When I was pregnant with Gail, your sister, I had to stay in bed for months so I would not miscarry. There were a lot of complications. I didn't want to go through that ever again, but your dad always wanted another child. I didn't want another child at first, I was so scared. Sandi, will you please forgive me? I can't imagine my life without you now. You are such a joy to me. I just had to tell you my truth."

Immediately, I wrapped my arms around my mother. We cried together. There was never a thought in my mind growing up that my mother felt this way. Well, perhaps during my rebellious years when I was the devil with horns. Honestly, I wouldn't have blamed her anyway. I always felt love and acceptance from her. I could completely understand how she felt because of the revelation I had received when Brandon's professor revealed his rejection from the womb. It all made since now. My mom didn't want me while she was pregnant, so that is why all these years I have battled with someone to love me and accept me for me. I almost aborted Brandon; therefore, he felt rejection. When I was pregnant with King, my prayer was for King to be a girl. I didn't want to bring another boy into this world that would have to pay the price for the sin in my bloodline. Another son being born with this eye disorder was my fear. Wow!

Consider Mary the mother of Jesus: She was approached by an angel, telling her she would bear a child and bring forth the Messiah. Yet, she had never had an intimate relationship with any male. Imagine how she must have felt. I can only imagine her thoughts of trying to explain this to Joseph. *Well, Joseph you will never believe what just happened to me. An angel of the Lord, you know, big wings and all, appeared to me and told me I was going to have a baby. The angel even told me his name. Joseph, it was unbelievable.* Joseph probably would have sent her away, thinking she was crazy, except he encountered the same angel explaining what was going to happen.

Mary, while carrying Jesus, was rejected, mocked, shunned, isolated, feared for her life, abandoned, ridiculed, and I'm sure so much more. Jesus felt those feelings in Mary's womb. The Book of Hebrews says, "For we do not have a high priest who is unable to empathize with our weaknesses, but we have one who has been tempted in every way, just as we are—yet he did not sin" (4:15 NIV).

Jesus' blood shed at Calvary cancels every sickness, infirmity, and disease. His shed blood covers all our sins. Ephesians 1:7 says, "In Him we have redemption through His blood, the forgiveness of our trespasses, according to the riches of His grace" (NIV). The word *redemption* means "the action of saving or being saved from sin, error, or evil." We have been redeemed by Jesus. He is our saving grace.

I'm so glad King wasn't a girl; Bri is too.

Self-Awareness: I don't know what you are facing today. Perhaps, your mother had a troubled pregnancy like my mother and me. I am comforted by my heavenly Father's words in John 14:26, "But the Helper (Comforter, Advocate, Intercessor, Counselor, Strengthener, and Standby), the Holy Spirit, whom the Father will send in My name, He will teach you all things. And He will help you remember everything I have told you" (NKJV). Nothing we go through in life, if we have accepted Jesus as our personal Savior, will we ever have to face alone. His Spirit is within us, granting us strength and grace for the journey. What is Jesus speaking to you in this chapter? What is He trying to teach you? You may never know what your mother felt in her womb while carrying you. Regardless of what she felt, know this: because of Jesus, we can be free from addiction, depression, resentment, bitterness, hatred, anger, lust, pride, disease to please, fear, and rejection. Jesus knows how you feel. He bore those feelings on the cross so that you can be free. Today is your day to be free. Open your heart and let Him in.

Personal Lies: _____

_____

_____

_____

_____

_____

_____

Personal Truths: _____

_____

_____

_____

_____

_____

_____

Chapter 16

The Lioness

Rick and I are officially empty nesters now. At first, I wasn't handling this well . . . the circle that once was large has now dwindled to just five—Rick's mom and dad, my mom, and the two of us. Rick has such wisdom. He doesn't say a lot but when he speaks, he speaks such truth. He said, "Quiet never sounded so loud." It is so true. I can see why married couples leave each other after their children have left the house, if they don't take time to keep the passion in their relationship. I like Rick and he likes me back. That makes my heart happy. My momma always said, "Invest in your marriage, because your children will leave you; your husband won't." Well, at least my second one didn't.

We are adjusting, realizing that every day is truly a gift from God. Our circle is enlarging daily by the people our children are reaching for Jesus Christ in sharing His love. We are all part of God's great big family. But I miss my children deeply. My only consolation is they are pursuing their calling, and that makes my heart happy. Jesus gives us grace for every phase of the journey.

The lioness' family is called a pride. I know what that feels like. I take pride in my family, not with arrogance, but gratefulness for the God-fearing people they are. The lioness is extremely protective of her babies. So am I. I can't even imagine how Mary, the mother of Jesus, must have felt when she saw her Son being crucified. The days leading up to His death, trying to prepare His momma for His crucifixion, must have weighed heavily on Him. He knew His momma was going to witness His disciples betraying Him, selling Him out for 30 pieces of silver, and soldiers beating Him beyond recognition.

The flesh on His back was ripped; a spear was thrust into His side; a crown of thorns was pressed down upon His head. He was ridiculed and spit upon as He took His last dying breath on a rugged old cross.

Go here with me: Mary was kneeling at his feet, hearing him mumble, taking small deep breaths, enduring the severe pain. His hands and feet were torn open from his own weight when He was nailed to the cross, yet He knew this was His mission. Jesus had me on His mind . . . you, too. There was no hate or anger, no bitterness from the way His disciples treated him; only pure love. He had enough love to listen to the thief beside Him and pardon his sin. The thief didn't have to recite some lengthy scripture, pray, or meditate for hours. He simply cried out in his desperation, "Jesus, remember me." Jesus responded with, "See you in paradise, my friend, in a few hours." (Sandi's translation) My best friend, Jesus, my Savior, my Lord was born to die. Born to die for all people even though they may never accept Him as the Messiah, their Savior.

But we can't leave this beautiful story of love and life in a grave. If Jesus were just born to die, we would still be destined for a place called hell. It was customary in that region to punish people by crucifixion. It was the miraculous third-day resurrection that made His life worth paying the price. Mary must have thought her Son was dead. But she remembered His words of hope, because He said He would come back for her. Jesus is our only hope.

Sometimes self-pity tries to settle in when things don't go the way I think they should, which is ridiculous. I created nothing but chaos. He created the world out of nothing. He trumps me, always.

In this season of my life, I was tired. The business was extremely exhausting. As a staffing agency, we find people work. Placing the right candidate at the right position is hard enough, but when the people take our time, and then choose not to show up, that is what makes this career so stressful. We are depending upon humanity to go to work. Rick's sweet parents were aging and demanding more attention, and we were feeling stretched. Our business numbers had dropped. After many years of having a full staff, we found ourselves just the way the business had started—just the two of us.

I would answer the phone and put the caller on hold. Only to pick the phone back up and change my voice to sound like another person. It was funny, especially when there was a complaint and they wanted to speak to the manager. I was the manager, the janitor, the front desk receptionist, and the recruiter. I was all things to mankind, and I was tired. I was done.

Have you ever felt done? This lioness wanted to hide in the woods and take a nap, a very long nap. A lioness is known to be the hunter and provide the food for her babies. They nurture their pride to be strong and grow up healthy, to fight against the enemies who would seek to devour them. Sounds familiar! As a woman and a mother, I understand this!

Well, I was exhausted. This was a long, weary season. For six years, we felt like we were treading water, fighting not to go under. Having to take care of his parents, we knew we wouldn't be able to go out of the country, or the beach to take a vacation, so we invested in a hot tub. We placed it in our backyard—our very own "staycation." It was in March of 2015. We got in the hot tub one evening, and I began to tell Rick my truths. I knew if I told Rick my truths it would probably add extra pressure to his life, and I didn't want that. I had almost lost him in 2014 due to a toxic gallbladder. He was in ICU for four days. All the pressure of the business, his parents, and his sickness were weighing on me. I am extremely protective of Rick and his health. I'm sure it must have to do with what my daddy went through. But I had to get some things off my chest. I needed relief. The stress was making me different. I was tired all the time, and my usual happy self was on the shelf. I wasn't getting to speak much into the lives of girls, which was my passion and purpose, so I felt my dreams were dying. I felt I was dying inside.

Rick listened tentatively in the hot tub as I begin to express myself. With such kindness, he could see and sense my need for help. "Ok", he said, "let me take some pressure off you and let me go in early. Take six months and back off from being in the business." I was so grateful; I could feel the pressure lifting off. He left the hot tub, and I continued my conversation with my Jesus. Yeah, I talk to Him anywhere and everywhere.

What was so cool about Jesus was, about 10 years ago, Rick and I were members of the country club. We love to golf, so we thought it would be a great stress reliever. But because the business was down, we had to let our membership go. We were sad, but we were always ready and willing to do whatever we needed to do to keep the business running.

Since we had to stay close to take care of our aging parents, we renewed our membership. When Rick told me the number, it was the same as we had from the past membership. I felt my sweet Savior speak to me as only He can: "This is the beginning of restoration for your drought." He was speaking life into our dry bones. We would see the sun shine again. A promise.

Back to the hot tub: I was having my conversation with Jesus with my self-pity attitude, because things weren't going my way. He said to me so sweetly: "What are you sitting in"?

I said, "a hot tub."

"What did I restore back to you that you enjoyed so much"?

I responded, "The country club membership."

"Do you have a nice house?"

"Yes, Sir."

"Are you driving nice cars?"

"Yes, Sir."

"Do you have nice clothes?"

"Yes, Sir."

"Then stop whining, my Israelite. Be content with what you have. I have never failed you, and I never will."

I put my head down like a scolded two-year-old who just got a spanking from acting spoiled and having a temper tantrum.

Look at the words self-pity. Self obviously is referring to an individual like you and me. When you add pity to self, self-pity translates into an individual being absorbed with a victim mentality. Pity means "disappointment, misfortune of events, wanting extreme sympathy." Self-pity was the garment I was wearing. Self-pity is not attractive. Imagine a lioness waking up one morning looking at her cubs saying, I really don't want to hunt food for you today. You just need to figure this out for yourself and go find your own food for survival. Perhaps you had a mother like that; you don't have to be like her. Find someone who is a successful mother and ask her to teach you how to be a good mother. That is biblical—the older generation teaches the younger generation.

The lion, the male, is the protector of the pride. Jesus, the Lion of Judah, is your protector, provider, defender, helper, and supplier of more than enough of whatever you need. He is your healer of a broken heart. You may be asking yourself, *but if Jesus is so great,* why did He allow such bad things to happen to me when I was a child? Why did my pastor, who was supposed to be my spiritual resemblance of Jesus, molest me? Where was my mother when I needed her to kiss my wounds when people hurt me? Where was Jesus when I lost my five-month old child to SIDS? Why did He give me a child only to die from a drunk driver and be taken from me? Why did he give me a vision of a business and it failed? Why did he spare me and allow my whole family to be killed by a mob while living in another country as missionaries? Why did he allow me to get married for two years and my husband get killed in the line of fire oversees? Why did he allow my son's wife to die in a car wreck leaving me with three children to raise?

I don't have all the answers. I don't know why bad things happen to good people, but what I do know is in this life we are guaranteed troubles. Troubles started in the Garden of Eden. The great news is, Jesus, the Lion of Judah, roars victory over you in the wilderness. He has and will give you the strength to overcome any obstacle life throws at you. I know this to be true. If He will do it for me, He will do it for you, too.

I don't know why Jesus gives me visuals when I pray, but He does. I will see faces of people and begin to pray over them in the Spirit. Like a movie, I see them right before my eyes. One time recently, I was praying for a dear friend. She and her family had just suffered a tremendous loss in their family. I saw her sitting in Jesus' lap weeping. Suddenly, she started beating His chest in anger telling Him she was so mad at Him and why did He allow this tragedy to happen. "Why didn't you save him from his death?" She kept beating the chest of Jesus. He just kept holding her tightly, bringing her closer to His chest. She kept pulling back in anger, but He kept pulling her closer. I began to weep with her while praying over her. "Oh Jesus, please, Sir, comfort her grieving heart. Give her peace in exchange for her despair." He asked me to call her and tell her what I saw while praying. Please tell her, "It's okay she is mad, even furious with Me. I can handle her anger and love her anyway. One day she will understand." I did. We cried together.

I don't know what you are facing in life. Disappointment, perhaps, is the only garment you put on every morning. You can't forgive God for being so cruel to you. May I ask you to consider this thought? Being angry with God isn't going to bring that person back. Being disappointed with God isn't going to change your circumstances.

I could have stayed in the victim, self-pity mental attitude with all the stuff life threw at me. But I chose not to. You can, too. After my first divorce, I went to a therapist. He told me, after his thorough observation, that my self-esteem and self-worth were beaten down; it was as if I had been raped multiple times. I couldn't even look people in the face. I would keep my head down because I thought people wouldn't accept all my shame.

Earlier, I mentioned I wanted to be a psychologist, to get my doctorate and help people. Since I didn't fulfill my education in college, I pursued life coaching. I went to Zig Ziglar's Educational School in Tampa, in 1999. I received my life-coaching certification. In 2014, I wanted to further my coaching, so I received my certification in family and divorce mediation. Recently, I started a coaching session called, G3p—the Genesis Project, the beginning of something great. This title came from Genesis 3. Why didn't I take it from Genesis 1, the beginning? The answer is because chapter 3 is the chapter describing the fall of man, the separation between God and His creation. He has asked me to be the one to introduce His children to His Son Jesus, the bridge to Him.

I have a mantle on my life to teach people how to live with Jesus. It would be my honor to have the privilege of introducing you to Jesus and teaching you how to live with Him. I promise you, you will never be the same. There is a disclaimer: You will still have troubles, but at least you won't have to walk through life alone. Once you accept Jesus as your Savior, acknowledge you need Him, just like the thief on the cross, and then He will make His home in your heart. Heaven will be your eternal home. This isn't a fairytale. It can be your personal truth. Usually, if it's too good to be true, it is. Well, this Jesus I have just described to you may sound too good to be true. But, I know He is real. I can testify to you for myself that once I was blind, but now I see.

My prayer and hope for you, is to enlighten you to open your eyes and see all that God has in store for you, and to encourage you to start believing again. When you start believing what your Creator says about you, you will act differently. When you fill your mind with His truths, darkness must flee. There were times when I felt such a demonic presence around me at nights that I would sleep with the Word on my chest and praise music in my ears. What you put in comes out. If you put the words of Jesus in you, you will shine like Jesus around you. Let me encourage you to talk with Him, anywhere and everywhere—in the car on the way to work. Walk with Him, like He so desired with Adam and Eve—when the sun comes up, in the cool of the evening, and at the grocery store. If you are mad at Him, like my mom and I were, scream at Him, if you need to; He can handle it. He came to this earth, left His deity, to have a relationship with you. He gets you. He knit your fibers together. He ordains your steps. He has every hair on your head numbered. He knows your concerns, frustrations, dreams, desires, and disappointments, and He wants to help you through life. He can and will restore what the Enemy of your soul has stolen. No, he won't bring my daddy back; neither will He bring back the one you are grieving over. Please stop believing your lies.

Maybe you battle with being good enough. You think there is no way Jesus would ever use you to help others. Well, let's look at the ones Jesus used for His Kingdom: Moses stuttered, Noah got drunk, Jacob was a deceiver, David was an adulterer, Paul plotted to kill Christians, Rahab was a prostitute, Martha was jealous of Mary, Peter betrayed Jesus, and Sarah laughed at the promise of God. There are so many more examples I could share with you. I just want you to see, you don't have to be perfect to accept Jesus. Jesus qualifies you.

I heard this joke about a woman who died and went to heaven. Before entering the gate, St. Peter greeted her with this question. He said, "Welcome to heaven. Before you can enter in, you must first spell a word. Please spell the word, love."

The woman was so excited, she clapped her hands and began to jump up and down and said, "Of course, I love the word love, and she began spelling it out loud—L-O-V-E." A few minutes later, St. Peter said he needed to run an errand and asked if she could watch the gate for newcomers. "Of course," she said.

While standing, waiting patiently, suddenly, she sees her ex-husband. He said, "What are you doing here?"

She responded, "Well, I was wondering the same about you." Reluctantly, she thought for a moment, and then said: "St. Peter had to run errands and asked me to oversee those who enter heaven." She said, "Before you are able to enter, you first must spell a word." She said, "Your word to spell is Czechoslovakia."

Aren't you so grateful that Jesus accepts us all just like we are and all He wants from us is to just love Him back. That's really all He is wanting from us is complete surrender. May I encourage you today not to allow one more moment to pass you by before you say "yes" to Jesus.

If you choose to accept Jesus as your Lord and Savior, like the thief on the cross, say this simple prayer with me:

Jesus, I confess and acknowledge I need a Savior.
Please come into my heart, so I can
make heaven my eternal home.
I choose to love You back, starting right now.
Thank You for forgiving me and granting me courage
to forgive others.
Thank You for making Yourself real to me as I
become real with You. Amen.

John 15:5 says, "I am the vine, you are branches. . . . Apart from me you can do nothing" (NIV). Please don't wait another minute. There is more to life than this. His name is Jesus.

I would love to hear from you. If you accepted Jesus Christ as your Lord and Savior, please contact me. I would love to hear your story, and if by chance, I can't meet you personally in this life, I want to meet you at the gate. By the way, you won't have to spell a word...

Then you will know the truth, and the truth will set you free.

—JESUS

**For information on how to contact
Sandi King Kramer
for Life Coaching or Speaking:**

website: www.sandikramer.tv
email: Sandi@SandiKramer.tv
Twitter: @Sandi_Kramer
Instagram: SandiKingKramer
Facebook: SandiKingKramer